S0-ACR-089

FLORIDA STATE
UNIVERSITY LIBRARIES

SEP 20 2000

TALLAHASSEE, FLORIDA

ELEVEN STORIES HIGH

Eleven Stories High

Growing Up in Stuyvesant Town,
1948–1968

Corinne Demas

State University of New York Press

F
128.68
.S78
D46
2000

frontispiece:
Tricycle riding in the Oval, 1949

Published by
State University of New York Press, Albany

© 2000 Corinne Demas

All rights reserved

Printed in the United States of America

No part of this book may be used or reproduced in any manner whatsoever without
written permission. No part of this book may be stored in a retrieval system or
transmitted in any form or by any means including electronic, electrostatic, magnetic
tape, mechanical, photocopying, recording, or otherwise without
the prior permission in writing of the publisher.

For information, address State University of New York Press
State University Plaza, Albany, New York 12246

Production by Dana Foote
Marketing by Fran Keneston

All photographs are from
the author's private collection.

Library of Congress Cataloging-in-Publication Data

Demas, Corinne.
Eleven stories high : growing up in Stuyvesant Town, 1948–1968 / Corinne Demas.
p.   cm.
ISBN 0–7914–4629–8 (alk. paper)
1. Demas, Corinne—Childhood and youth. 2. Stuyvesant Town (New York,
N.Y.)—Biography. 3. Women—New York (State)—New York—Biography. 4. New
York (N.Y.)—Biography. 5. Stuyvesant Town (New York, N.Y.)—Social life and
customs—20th century. 6. New York (N.Y.)—Social life and customs—20th
century.
I. Title.

F128.68.S78 D46 2000
813'.54—dc21
[B]   00–022443

FOR MY FATHER

CONTENTS

Contents

Contents

ILLUSTRATIONS

The view from Apartment 9B

PROLOGUE

When I was a child, growing up in Stuyvesant Town, in New York City, I did not know any women who live as I do now, in a place like this, with a view like this from their window. I am a stranger even to my imagination then.

I look out from my study now at a stretch of imperfect lawn, a wooded hillside, and in the distance beyond, an ellipse of a pond, nearly hidden in the trees. In winter when the pond is frozen, I can see silhouettes of skaters gliding across the ice. In the green seasons even the hillside is lost behind leaves. It's so quiet here now I can hear the brushing of the wind through the white pines, the purr of the furnace, the clink of my dog's collar on the wooden floor as he stretches out at my feet. Only one car has passed on the road since I sat at my desk this morning, leaving not a whisper of itself behind.

It took decades of distance for me to see Stuyvesant Town at all, to form any notion of its identity. Stuyvesant Town was as familiar, as unremarkable to me as my own face. It wasn't until I began thinking about my children's childhoods, that I began to take note of what was distinctive about my own. And I came to see that Stuyvesant Town was not just a place where I happened to grow up, but a way of life.

I've spent the past twenty-five years writing fiction. Wisps of my real past have served as inspiration or provided detail, but I've been wary of autobiography and never embraced it in my stories. To prod at the past is a frightening occupation for a writer who has spent most of her career secure in the privacy that fiction affords. To write about

Stuyvesant Town I had to revisit it in my mind unchaperoned and confront it on paper on its own terms.

When you write fiction you create the truths and build the lives of your characters to serve your story. In a memoir the characters are real people, whose stories strain against your design. The easiest way to impose order on the past is to relate it chronologically. But chronology is often at odds with memory, for rarely does our past reveal itself to us in sequence. Some memories lay claim to us, while others are recondite and evanescent. In this book I've aimed to follow the process of memory rather than the conventions of chronology, and chosen to recapture some of my Stuyvesant Town childhood through a collection of observations inspired by topic rather than the course of time.

There are many stories in Stuyvesant Town, as many stories as there are lives, most, like mine, undistinguished by fame or fortune, trauma or tragedy. But even if this were fiction, I wouldn't want to invent something extraordinary for the character who would be me as a child. For these are scenes from a childhood that was free of hardship, a childhood that was privileged, and—dare I say it?—relatively happy, and a portrait of a place, Stuyvesant Town, that was a comfortable, middle-class community, a utopia of the Fifties.

Acknowledgments

My thanks to the many people who helped this project along the way, among them: the folks at MetLife, including Pat Brady, Public Relations, Paul Latimer, Recreation Director, and Daniel B. May, Company Archivist; Third Street Music School Settlement; Marge Kolb, Hunter College High School Alumnae/i Association; Diane De-Veaux, Librarian and Geraldine Cobbs, Assistant Librarian, Hunter College High School Library; Elsa Okun Rael; Rebecca Davis; and my colleagues at Mt. Holyoke College.

I am grateful for the support and encouragement of my writing group; my agent, Tracey Adams; my friends from Stuyvesant Town and beyond, especially Elaine and Chuck vonBruns, Zane Kotker, and the Weiss Family; my cousin, Carole Demas; my son and daughter; and, as always, my husband.

Special thanks to my editor, Dale Cotton, for his wisdom and enthusiasm, and to Jane and Alan Carey, for being there for me.

I
Stuyvesant Town

To begin at the end.

It took me five years after my mother's death to finally break the lease, empty the closets, and double lock the door for the last time. Of course I looked back as I left (it's only in stories that people don't) at the fourteen-story-high brick wall, punctuated by windows, where my childhood had taken place, that modest aerie.

The last night, after a hot day of packing, my husband, daughter, and I were walking back to the apartment from dinner at a local deli. In the distance I saw a family with a white dog cute as a stuffed toy. I was marveling that people were walking a dog in a place where residents were forbidden to own them, and was thinking about how I had longed for a dog all the years of my childhood, my great unrequited wish. My daughter pulled us towards the dog, and just as the humans were coming close enough for me to see their faces, the woman broke free from the group and came running towards me, crying out my nickname, "Cory!"

It was my childhood friend Marla, grown up, a wife, a mother. She lived out of town and was visiting her mother who still lived here. That she recognized me in spite of the disguise of twenty-five years was a miracle. Our eight-year-old daughters looked so much like ourselves from our past the eye could morph the years between. We all went up to her mother's apartment, a one-bedroom now, more appropriate for her widowed lifestyle, but the same credenza along the wall. (My family did not own one, but it was a word I loved to pronounce as a child; it invoked Venice itself.) While we talked our daughters did gymnastic tricks in the small, overdecorated living room space, my friend's mother insisting it was all right, I needn't worry about them breaking anything: the indulgence of a grandmother. We jumped on the sofa when we were eight (and our mothers yelled at us) but we didn't do gymnastics—girls didn't do things like that, then. Both our daughters now live in houses with stairs, play on grass, own dogs, take for granted what we were forbidden. They wonder at the elevators we traveled in every day, at the acres of playgrounds, at the chain fence that separates the pavement from anything green, at the rules and habits that govern the lives of Stuyvesant Town.

Stuyvesant Town. If this were a novel you would think I made it up. Imagine some giant hand leveling eighteen square blocks of Manhattan tenements, and in their place constructing a utopia of brick apartment buildings laid out around a large central green called the Oval. The only streets, four semicircular drives, one on each side of the perimeter, and a maze of paved walking paths and twelve fenced playgrounds, some with swings and slides, some with basketball hoops, some simply square open spaces. The focal point of the Oval, a fountain with three spires of water, still tempting the children to wet their feet, but that wasn't allowed (and there were guards to see to it). On hot afternoons, in some of the playgrounds, huge showers were turned on over an area with a center drain, and we children ran, screaming, through the icy water.

Stuyvesant Town encompasses all the territory from Fourteenth Street to Twentieth Street, from First Avenue east to the East River—seventy-five acres. Peter Cooper Village, similar, but slightly more affluent (the apartments have two bathrooms and larger living rooms) runs from Twentieth Street to Twenty-third. East River Drive, an elevated highway, separates the complex from the river itself. Underneath what we called the viaduct, is a long parking lot, cheaper than the underground garages in Stuyvesant Town itself. It was there that my father parked, and our car was always covered with soot that fell from the great metal underpinnings of the highway, and decorated by the pigeons who nested there. Every time when my father went to pick up the car for our weekend excursions he would shake his fist at the birds, yell at them, and laugh. Then he would take a great feather duster from the trunk of the car and brush the soot from the windshield and the door handles. He was always studying the underside of the viaduct, trying to figure out where the pigeons were most likely to roost so he could avoid parking there.

"I'll outsmart them yet," he said. But he never did.

Stuyvesant Town had been built in a part of Manhattan that had been filled-in marshy tidelands of the East River. Known as the Gas House District, it was an area of tenements, commercial buildings and gas tanks, economically depressed by 1940, and targeted for redevelopment by Robert Moses, New York City Park Commissioner. The project was taken on by Metropolitan Life Insurance Company (now called MetLife), who had built a similar development in the Bronx, called Parkchester. The name Stuyvesant Town was selected to give the 25,000 residents a whiff of historical connection, for in the late eighteenth century the riverfront homestead of Peter Stuyvesant III, the great-grandson of the Dutch governor, had stood on the spot.

Stuyvesant Town was a gargantuan undertaking—begun in 1944—which involved relocating three thousand families and demolishing five hundred buildings. Construction costs were over a hundred million dollars, and the project consumed 40,000 tons of steel and 36,500,000 bricks. The first families moved in, in 1947.

Unlike the vast city public housing projects in ghetto neighborhoods, meccas of despair, Stuyvesant Town was a middle-class community where little girls took piano lessons and were expected to go to college. If our fathers weren't doctors or dentists, lawyers or school principals, they worked in offices and on hot days still wore their jackets home from work, with their ties just loosened. If our mothers worked at all, they were teachers. When families got wealthier they bought homes in Scarsdale or Darien or moved up to apartments in Peter Cooper. Some just stayed and kept their money in any one of the many banks nearby on First Avenue. By the time I was in high school there were more elderly residents, and when they died *Town and Village,* the local weekly newspaper, sometimes reported their estates. A hundred thousand dollars, two hundred thousand dollars, half a million! My mother read these articles aloud at the dinner table.

"It just goes to show you," she said, she who cherished the modest life. For me the message was a different one. These people were socking away their money while they lived in tiny apartments and lugged shopping carts full of groceries home from D'Agostino's and shopping carts full of dirty laundry down to the laundromat where they sat with the rest of us watching their clothes slosh around in a foamy sea through the portholes of the washing machines. Were they all mad?

When I had been born, my parents lived on the Upper West Side in a real New York apartment building with an awning and an elevator man. I was as fascinated by this, as if I had spent those first two years of my life in an exotic country. The noise of Seventy-third Street below kept my father awake at night. In Stuyvesant Town, the one-way curved drive had little traffic: a few delivery trucks, a swish of taxi cabs, and on Sundays a few private cars picking up families for outings.

Everyone who lived in Stuyvesant Town was white. Most everyone in my building was Jewish. Families I knew numbered one or two children, occasionally three, except for one Catholic family who had five.

It was only the most fortunate families—nine thousand of them—who got apartments in Stuyvesant Town. When Stuyvesant Town was first ready for occupancy, there were more than 200,000 inquiries, and preference was given to World War II veterans and their families, who made up ninety-eight percent of the original tenants. Most of them were young couples, like my parents, with little kids. The waiting lists were long and you had to pass muster: inspectors visited your current dwelling to see that you'd make a suitable tenant.

A number of my childhood friends still live in Stuyvesant Town. Some occupy the apartments they were raised in—their surviving parents tucked away in smaller apartments, or in nursing homes. Some moved away to the suburbs or the Upper West Side and then were drawn back again. Some, like me, move far enough away so they'll be safe from the pull.

In Stuyvesant Town everything was homogeneous, symmetrical, and orderly. There were eight apartments on each floor, four two-bedroom, two one-bedroom, and two coveted three-bedroom. There were fourteen floors, but the first floor was called "Terrace" (T on the elevator button panel) and the second floor, where you exited at the back of the building on the level above the parking garage, was called, perversely, "Main" (M). This eliminated the unfortunate thirteenth floor. We lived in apartment 9B, but we were actually on the eleventh story.

Ours was a prime apartment, looking south over the Oval. An identical building faced us across the Oval, but it was close to Fourteenth Street, while we were close to Twentieth so there was enough space between for the sun to fill our apartment and goad my mother's geraniums to bloom continuously on the window sills.

The symmetry of Stuyvesant Town bewildered people. Once some old army friend of my father, who was perhaps a bit drunk, came to visit and got lost in the maze of buildings. We heard him bellowing up from the center oval, "Nick Demas, where the hell do you live?" His voice echoed against the buildings, to my mother's horror. Even the natives sometimes got confused, though not the children. In an episode that sounds like familiar fiction, but was in fact quite true, a father in my building went home by mistake to the identical building across the way. He went upstairs in the identical elevator, got off at his floor, went to his apartment, where the door was unlocked (this was the fifties: doors were unlocked during the day so the kids could run freely from one apartment to another) and walked in. He wondered if his wife had gotten new furniture, shouted "Hello!" to her, and a strange woman screamed in the bathroom.

Our apartments were all alike. They had the same layouts, the same sand-colored metal cabinets in the kitchen, sand-colored porcelain fixtures in the bathroom, tan walls (unless you paid an exorbitant fee to have them painted other than Stuyvesant Town "decorator" colors) and the same wooden parquet floors, one foot squares, four boards across. The floors were attractive, but regulations required you kept them carpeted. If you didn't have wall-to-wall carpeting you could see edges of the real wood.

A friend of mine who grew up in Stuyvesant Town believes the sameness made people crazy—the fact that everything appeared to be identical, but on closer inspection, really wasn't. I disagree. For children, especially, I think the sameness was comforting. When you went to visit a friend's apartment the floorplan was reassuringly familiar—the bathroom was in the same place, your friend's bedroom was the same size as your own. The layout of buildings, playgrounds, walks and drives, was all predictable, once you mastered the design. As a child you grew up seeking out subtle differences, you noticed details.

If Stuyvesant Town was bland, that just made the world outside it more brilliant. The variety of textures of buildings and stores and restaurants in the great city beyond seemed dazzling to me as a child. I'd walk along First Avenue like a tourist in a foreign bazaar. When I got home, Stuyvesant Town always seemed, in contrast, serene. No doubt the deprivations of Stuyvesant Town made me acutely sensitive to my surroundings when I was in the country. The limitless variety of plants, the irregularities of terrain, a feast for my senses. No child reared in Stuyvesant Town ever takes nature for granted.

Stuyvesant Town walls were, I always said, thin, but I don't think that's true. They were real plaster, probably thicker than modern sheetrock. The problem was their conductivity of sound, perhaps because all the moldings and doors were metal. (Stuyvesant Town was ideally fireproof. If a fire broke out, you simply shut the door.)

We lived intimately with our neighbors. We could hear them walking around and talking. We knew what program they were listening to on the radio, what they were watching on T.V. The steam pipe in the bathroom, carried children's laments and mothers' nagging—over tooth brushing, wiping, flushing, and washing—up and down the entire column of Apartment Bs. Children practiced their instruments in the evenings and if you were waiting for the elevator in the hall you'd likely be serenaded by several pianos, a violin or two, a clarinet, and an occasional trombone. The Smiths next door in Apartment C, the one-bedroom, did not have children, so our piano was not on "their wall."

Our kitchen, a lopsided pentagon, fitted neatly against the kitchen of Apartment A, at a right angle to ours. One evening our neighbor, Murray, came home and complained to his wife that he had gotten to work ten minutes early because she had told him the wrong time in the morning. It turned out that when he had called out "What time is it, honey?" his wife was in the hall, throwing garbage down the incinerator, and my mother, in our kitchen, had answered, mistaking his voice for my father's. In our house all the clocks were kept ten minutes ahead in order to help us get to places on time. (A trick that never worked, for I always counted on the extra ten minutes and to this day am thrown off by clocks that tell "true" time.)

We could see into each other's apartments as well. The buildings were H shaped, so all apartments could look catty-corner into others, and some of the apartments looked directly across into ones on the other side of the building. It was easiest to look into windows on floors below. I once saw a boy lying naked on the bed whom I recognized as a kid I'd see bike riding. His body was pale and slender, and he was so innocent of my watching him I felt ashamed. A boy I had a crush on lived in the building across the drive. I knew which block of windows was his family's, guessed which window was his room. It was too far away for me to see in, but I knew what time his shade was pulled down, what time his light went out. I fantasized that he watched my window, too, though I suspected he didn't know, or care, who I was.

There were people whose lives I had glimpses of whom I never saw in person, never heard. There were people whom I heard, whose apartments were out of sight. Sometimes I could match a familiar voice with someone who rode on my elevator or someone I ran into. Some families' interactions were in the background my whole childhood—the children getting older as I did—sometimes voices disappeared and new ones took their places. If I was a voyeur and an eavesdropper, so was everyone else. I guarded the little privacy I had fiercely, but sometimes I used the theater of neighbors as a weapon in squabbles with my mother. "Lower your voice," was her constant refrain in my childhood. "I don't care who hears me," my retort.

All of the windows in our apartment, except one, faced south onto the Oval. The window in the back bedroom, the room where the television resided, faced north, and gave me a glimpse of the spire of the Empire State Building and other uptown skyscrapers, a reminder of the world beyond Stuyvesant Town. In spite of conscious efforts to call it "the den" (which raised images for me of a wood-paneled study in a suburban house) this room was forever referred to as "the backroom." Cool and dark, approached through a little hallway, it was like an appendage to our apartment. (In fact it was the second bedroom from the one-bedroom next door.)

Everything in Stuyvesant Town was regulated and manicured. Order always prevailed. The playgrounds, all surrounded by metal fences too high to climb over, were locked up at night, although it was never clear what was being kept out. During the day the children inside the playgrounds looked like zoo animals, caged in.

We children enjoyed most playing outside of the spaces allotted to us. We dug in the narrow strips of dirt between the cobblestones around the benches. We wrote messages with chalk on the stone bases of the flagpoles. We were constantly lured by the unpaved areas behind the thigh-high chain fences. There were lawns and patches of ivy and small hillsides between buildings where rhododendron and azalea grew. The guards who patrolled the area and were paid to protect us, we saw as the enemy. I can remember the terror invoked by the cry "Guard!" when I was playing with some friends under some shrubbery on the forbidden side of fence. We ran back to the safety of our mothers who were chatting on the benches along the playground and were oblivious to our narrow escape.

Only when it snowed did we fearlessly challenge the boundaries. Early in the morning on a snowday that had closed the schools, my friends and I, with our snowsuits on top of our pajamas, stamped out our names in the snow right out in the center of the Oval lawn in letters so big we could read them from my apartment windows. If it stayed cold, they'd remain there for days. As it warmed up, tufts of green would start showing through the thinnest places, our names would grow illegible, and finally they'd disappear so completely into the green lawn that it was hard to believe they had ever been there at all.

II

ELEVATORS

A child who grows up eleven stories in the air has a peculiar relationship with the outdoors. From the bedroom window it was the sky that was my landscape, not the ground. The trees—saplings when I was a child, now six stories high—were seen from above, their trunks invisible under a great territory of leaves. It was as easy to touch a cloud as the earth below.

In the morning we could not step outdoors to see what kind of a day it was. In winter if you stuck your hand out the window the air always felt colder than it was, compared with the steam heat rising from the radiator beneath your arm. In summer the brick-baked air outside the window was always hotter than the air at street level, where there was shade from buildings and trees.

"Look out and see what everyone's wearing," my mother would advise me each morning so I'd know how to get dressed. Once I made it outside I'd never go all the way back upstairs to change. (Mothers threw down ice-cream money or forgotten skate keys to waiting children—after yelling, "stand back, stand out of the way!"—but nothing as big as a sweater.) We told the weather by the way the people wore their clothes, by the way they walked. I watched for subtle clues. Even from eleven stories up you could tell if people were huddled in their coats, their chins buried in mufflers, or if their coats were open, their hats off.

There were two elevators in my building—two in every Stuyvesant Town building. They were identical elevators with shiny metal enamel interiors: red, green, and blue. We had gotten green, worst luck. The elevator was our single passageway to the entire world outside our apartment, our passageway back home. The only time we took the stairs was at Halloween for trick or treating, and one time when the power had gone out. Into these boxes we disappeared twice, sometimes four times, sometimes six or eight times a day. Unless we were going away overnight, it was always an even number of trips.

Magicians in shows stuff rabbits in boxes and open the lid to fluttering doves. Our boxes transformed us not at all. We left them as we had entered them, our journey never altering us, only repositioning our altitude. Still, the concept spawned fantasies. I imagined a magical metamorphosis—I'd step in the elevator a child and come out a grownup, or emerge as someone different or transformed into something else.

We knew our neighbors by their floors, as people in small towns associate their neighbors with their houses. It's possible there were some tenants I never saw—their entrances and exits never coinciding with mine—but in two decades I had built up a catalogue of faces, each face connected with a numbered floor. Though practically identical, each floor took on the character of its occupants. Some floors buzzed with families with little kids, others seemed sedate. There were people we knew by name and floor, and nameless people we knew by floor alone: the blond divorcee on Seven, the parochial school kids on Three, the man-in-the-wheelchair on Two. Weekday mornings there were the regulars, and I could tell how early or late I was by whom I was riding with. The elevator went straight up to Twelve and progressed downwards, collecting people as it went, stopping, on a school morning, at least five times. All conversations were public. People on lower floors had to pick up in medias res and gather and disseminate gossip faster. At the lobby everyone dispersed and conversations were suspended till the next morning's ride. Between 7 and 9 A.M. the elevator was nearly filled with people, standing erect, usually facing the door. Later, the pace slowed and the elevator had a more informal look. The space was taken up by bicycles, strollers, carriages, shopping carts, doll carriages, tricycles, push toys, pull toys, and sometimes toddlers splayed out on the floor.

By the time I got my new English three-speed racing bike, a Raleigh Sports, the carriage room, which had been good enough for my Huffy Convertible, had been hit too often by thieves and vandals. I kept my bicycle in my bedroom, arm's reach from my bed, and took it up and down the elevator when I went riding after school. It was a trick to hold the outside elevator door open while you wheeled in your bike, a trick to turn it a half circle inside the elevator so you could exit quickly at T. Two bikes and a stroller would fill the place up. People waiting at lower floors would either shake their heads and wait for the next elevator, or nimbly wedge themselves in among the wheels and kids.

In the morning the elevator was clean and bare. By afternoon there was a forgotten mitten propped under the banister, chewing gum stuck to the wall, juice spilled in the corner, and a tiny trail of white powdered detergent that had leaked out of a shopping cart on its way to the laundromat.

The elevator shaft was an airless, lightless no-man's-land. It was possible to climb up on the railing that ran at waist height around the car and balance yourself in the corner. You'd be careful not to stick your fingers through the open grate around the ceiling edge because they could be sliced off, but you could cling to the walls and peer out into the darkness of the shaft. Needless to say you could do this only if no grownup was in the elevator with you. There was a trap door in the ceiling of the elevator, an escape hatch for a disaster. Stories circulated about some kid who not only stuck his whole head out the hatch but had ridden up and down on top of the elevator. He either was mashed flat when the elevator got to the top of the shaft, tumbled off and was squished at the bottom, or had nothing happen to him at all. We weren't sure which.

The elevator was utterly predictable in its habits. It always ran at the same speed. When I and a friend were able to secure two elevators for elevator races, if we had a pure, unstopped run, we always arrived at the same time. The elevator always made the same groaning sound as its doors opened and shut, the same clicking as it passed each floor. It always obeyed our commands, though in my nightmares it sometimes went wild, stopping between floors, refusing to stop where I wanted to—worst of all, plummeting straight to the bottom, its cables shot. We often speculated what would happen if the cables broke. Rumor had it there was a giant spring at the bottom of the elevator shaft in case of such an emergency, and if you had started at Twelve and plunged straight down you would fly up to Three on the first bounce, drop down and bounce up to One before settling at the bottom. I imagined the elevator bursting through its roof and taking me away somewhere, this sulking beast condemned to its dark tunnel. Or rattling sideways in the shaft until it pushed its way through.

The elevator gave us children a sense of the kind of power only adults usually enjoyed. Simply by pressing a licorice-black button no bigger than a dime, we were able to move a room larger than our kitchen. We often pretended we were elevator operators, airplane pilots, or spacecraft commanders. There was always the temptation to push more buttons than necessary. When a grownup was around you had to satisfy yourself by pushing your one legitimate button half a dozen times. If you were alone you could push a button just as you left and send the elevator off to any destination of your choice. You could track it as it followed your command by watching the changing numerals behind the glass window in the panel on your floor. Some children hit all the elevator buttons as they left, condemning the next rider to stop at an endless number of floors, but though I longed to, I never dared. I imagined how serious the consequences could be: someone being rushed to the hospital could have their trip downstairs to the waiting ambulance so prolonged that they were dead by the time they reached the bottom.

When anyone moved or had deliveries of large furniture, the elevators would be clothed in khaki quilted pads, with a rectangular cut-out hole so you could still touch the button panel. These pads smelled of forest and were as comfy to lean against as your own bed.

If there were no grownups with us, my friends and I would hide behind them, or pretend we were crazy people locked up in a padded cell. We'd pound on the walls and scream "Let me out!" and when we arrived at T, dash past the shocked residents who had been waiting for the elevator in the lobby.

There were no service elevators in Stuyvesant Town buildings, and no service entrances. There was a democratic vision in this utopia: maids and masters, those served and those serving, all rode together.

I was warned to be wary of delivery men, even those whistling boys who carried dry-cleaning on their shoulder or the smiling delivery man from Gristede's. I was trained to check an elevator before I got into it, and not to ride with any man who wasn't a Daddy I knew. When I first rode the elevator alone when I was young, my mother saw me off, watched the numerals to see that I got down, then waited at the window for me to wave up to her. When I was old enough to navigate without her overseeing, I was constantly reminded of safety rules.

It was easy enough not to get into an elevator with a strange man, though I always pretended I was motivated by a change in plans, rather than have them think I mistrusted them. My dilemma came when I was on the elevator alone and then a strange man came on after me. There were a lot of floors between Nine and T, and if someone joined me I'd have to make a snap judgment. Would it be safer to ride all the way with this stranger or to get off when he got on? What if I got off and he chose to follow me? Which doorbell would I ring for help? Would anyone hear me if I cried out?

Sometime when I was in junior high school Stuyvesant Town installed convex mirrors in the elevators so you could quickly see the whole interior before you stepped on and wouldn't be surprised by someone hiding in the back corner. This safety measure confirmed all my fears. No one was ever murdered or held up or raped in the elevator in my building, but even in Stuyvesant Town you had to be constantly vigilant. After all, we lived in New York.

Having an elevator man—as some of my non-Stuyvesant Town friends did—could be an asset, but that depended entirely on the elevator man you happened to get. After my encounter in the elevator at Best & Co. I preferred the risks of a self-service elevator. My father was double-parked on the side street by the store, and I felt proud to be old enough to go upstairs to the girl's department on my own to pick up a coat that had been altered. The young man running the elevator in his smart uniform could have been a poster boy for West Point. He winked at me as I got on the car, my coat receipt tight in my hand, my hand inside my pocket. I was the only one on the elevator, an express. Somewhere, mid-journey, he stopped the elevator between floors and turned and grinned at me. Then he turned out the lights. I froze against the elevator wall. He didn't touch me or speak to me, he just laughed. Eventually he turned on the lights and brought me to my destination, winking at me as I left.

I got my coat. I took a local elevator back down. My father wondered what had taken so long, but I said nothing about what happened until I was home and, crying, told my mother what happened. She listened carefully and calmly. To reassure me, no doubt, she told me that he was probably just joking around and didn't mean to frighten me. Whether she ever called up Best & Co. and complained I don't know, but my next year's winter coat came from B. Altman's and it wasn't very long afterwards that Best & Co. suffered financial difficulties and that Fifth Avenue store shut its doors for good.

Stuyvesant Town may have been an innocent enclave in the fifties, but by the time I was a teenager it had been toughened up by the city around it. By the seventies the front lobbies were kept locked and residents were urged not to buzz in anyone they weren't expecting. An extra set of locks was added to all our apartment doors. The nickel-sized porthole that you swung open to see through was replaced by a fixed glass peephole that was like looking through the wrong end of a telescope. It was too tiny to poke a gun barrel through.

Our Stuyvesant Town apartment was burglarized only once, shortly before those double locks were installed. The thief took only cash and was very neat. In searching the apartment to get a total tally of the loss, my father came across money he had hidden years before for a possible emergency and forgotten about. Four fifty-dollar bills, folded twice, had been tucked in the back of the leather frame that held my father's Bronze Star medal from World War II. The frame lay on its back on the bookshelf on top of the World Scope Encyclopedia, an odd-brand, outdated set my parents had picked up cheap at a United States Post Office auction.

My father laughed. "That makes us forty dollars ahead," he said.

III

STORES

In the many interior acres of Stuyvesant Town there was not a single store. All commerce had been pushed to the peripheries. There were a few businesses on the Stuyvesant Town side of Fourteenth Street and First Avenue, but the real life of the city began across those streets.

The neighborhood that bordered Stuyvesant Town remained unchanged from the time before Stuyvesant Town had been created. You had only to look there—at the tenements, brownstones, and storefronts—to see what Stuyvesant Town had replaced. In Stuyvesant Town the traffic had been lulled, the tempo of the population had been moderated. In this way it resembled those pure residential suburban areas, where zoning kept commerce to its assigned territory. There were no billboards in Stuyvesant Town, no ads, no awnings.

Stuyvesant Town was clean as a hospital lab. Forces of men in brown uniforms were perpetually sweeping the sidewalks. An errant candy wrapper that some untutored child let slip from her fingers and that escaped her mother's watchful eye would have a short life on the smooth sidewalk before it was snatched up by a maintenance man. Some crews were armed with poles with needles at the end, designed to pin, pierce, and retrieve any scrap that did not belong.

When you stepped across First Avenue you were in another culture. There were crowds and bustle and disorder, dogs and cats who may not have belonged to anyone in particular, and litter of all varieties. In the gutter there were broken bottles and decayed fruit, and once I saw a mouse, not-quite-dead, in a discarded trap. The sidewalk was uneven and punctuated by cellar doors, often flapped open to reveal the catacombs of shops below, men with stacks of produce making their way up and down the steep steps. And the smells! Baking bread, garlic, garbage, paint, the sweat of people. In Stuyvesant Town I got no more than an occasional whiff of a neighbor's pot roast in the hall or perhaps a lingering hint of perfume in the elevator from the divorcee on Seven.

Delivery men made regular forays into Stuyvesant Town, bringing in the goods that the natives couldn't, or chose not to, carry home for themselves. The brown box of the UPS truck was as regular as the mail truck. Local businesses sent out "boys" (grown men, but always slender) on bicycles or giant tricycles with baskets mounted in front for groceries, laundry, dry-cleaning, and take-out food. They seemed like relics from a country village, from an era before the combustion engine.

The only permanent commercial intrusion in Stuyvesant Town was the Good Humor cart, stationed, for my entire childhood, on the corner of Stuyvesant Oval and Twentieth Street. The ice cream man's name was Sam. ("Sam, Sam, the ice-cream man," we chanted.) He was dressed in impeccable white—no smears of chocolate, no stains of orange ices—right down to his white buck shoes, although perhaps the years have whitened and starched his costume. His white cap, with a black visor, gave him a nautical air, so he resembled a sea captain, moored on the corner with his little craft. He was perpetually tan, and a dead ringer for Perry Como, though he never sang. He sat on a folding chair, listened to the baseball games on his portable radio, and smoked his cigar. I never saw him eat, not even one of his own ice-cream pops. He did not live in Stuyvesant Town and I have no idea how he got there and got home; he and his cart just appeared. He was at his post from spring through fall, and then he disappeared for the winter. He knew our names, knew our favorite flavors, and knew that the mothers were sitting on the benches not far away to oversee our selections. Icicles were forbidden ("colored sugar water") so I picked creamsicles (ice-cream mixed with sherbet) or ice-cream pops. Toasted Almond was a brave selection since some kids said it was vanilla that had been dropped in sawdust.

An ice-cream pop was one of the few treats in the world that had a consolation prize after the pleasure of eating it was over, for popsicle sticks were valuable currency. You'd hang around a younger kid who was innocent of this fact and snatch up the popsicle stick when the kid was done eating. When my mother wasn't looking I'd risk Germs and investigate the wire garbage can in the corner of the playground, in case there was a popsicle stick to extricate. I always had ambitious dreams of what I could build with them: jewelry boxes, doll's log cabins—although I never seemed to amass more than enough for a little toy raft.

Years later, I saw bags of popsicle sticks for sale in a craft store. They were real popsicle sticks, freshly minted, but they seemed counterfeit without the lingering stains of chocolate or strawberry. It was disillusioning that you could so easily acquire such a quantity without having to earn them by eating your way up to them, finding them, or bartering for them with your friends.

The businesses along First Avenue during the years of my childhood were as permanent as Stuyvesant Town itself. At the shoe store, our foot sizes were duly recorded on little cards kept as assiduously as our inoculation records at the pediatrician's office. There was a fluoroscope machine that enabled you to see right through your shoes and flesh to the bones of your feet, so you could tell how close your toes were to the ends of your shoes. My mother, with her typical scientific prescience, was convinced this machine was a health hazard and wouldn't let me put my feet in it, or even get too close. While other children's shoe sizing was determined by this newfangled device, my need for new footwear was entirely dependent on the archaic skill of Mr. Brunelle, prodding with his thumb on the toe of my oxford. If those other kids grew up to develop foot cancer, I haven't heard about it yet.

At Craig's, the bakery my mother frequented, we bought challah bread and seeded rye and pumpernickel, all sliced before our eyes by a machine with knives so sharp the loaf floated down over the blades and emerged, seemingly intact. For company we bought coffee rings, glazed, with pecans, that only grownups like, and cookies adorned with sprinkles. The bakery ladies, with plump, freckled arms, always gave me a sample cookie before they were weighed. Their hair was tethered in hairnets. At Craig's, ice cream cakes and birthday cakes were displayed behind cloudy, glass doors, and on the highest countertop there would be a wedding cake, a white palace, a concoction of icing that looked like lace. On the pinnacle was a painted plastic bride and groom, joined like Siamese twins, or a white bird covered with real feathers (some kids said they were from chickens, others said they were from doves). The cake boxes came in a flat stack and were folded, magically, into three dimensions. The string was dispensed from an endless reel mounted on the ceiling, and the bakery ladies always wound the string around the boxes twice in each direction and cut it tight enough so I could pluck it like a pretend guitar. On the way home I got to eat a piece of warm challah. I would peel off the shiny crust and then squeeze the white interior down to a lump in my fist.

The vegetable store on First Avenue was opened to the street across the whole front, and felt like an outdoor market. There was sawdust on the floor, and while my mother picked over the apples, I'd use the side of my shoe to mound up the sawdust and make little houses and hills and delineate streets. Fruits and vegetables were stockpiled side by side, a sort of United Nations of produce: bananas from Brazil, pineapples from Hawaii, oranges from Florida, potatoes from Maine. The scale bounced under their weight, my mother's eye on the clerk's fingers, to make sure he wasn't touching.

The Five and Ten on First Avenue had anything you could want to buy: pink rubber balls, wooden paddles with little balls attached to rubber strings, bottles of bubble soap with the blower floating inside, tubes of a translucent gluey substance that you wadded at the end of a straw and blew bubbles with, and when they came into fashion, Silly Putty and hula hoops. In the basement was an instant photo booth. You and a friend could squeeze in together. For a quarter you got a strip of sepia-toned photos—always goofy looking, even when you had resolved, at the outset, to look serious.

Most prevalent of all businesses adjacent to Stuyvesant Town were the banks. My mother had savings accounts at all of them, a common trend, for customers got prizes at each new bank opening, each new promotion. Bank gift electric can openers, toaster ovens, mixers, and lamps were ubiquitous in Stuyvesant Town apartments. Like most of the children I knew, I had my own savings account, a little book in a plastic sleeve that I kept in my top drawer under the lace-trimmed hankies I never used. Money that I had gotten as baby presents, money I got from relatives at Christmas, money I got for my birthday. I never withdrew it, only deposited it. When I was little I imagined that my money was actually there, set aside for me in the bank vault, "growing" like moss, a living demonstration of the miracles of compound interest. I lost my faith in banks when I learned that my money was only numbers in my book. Of course, if I asked for my money, I knew the bank would have to produce that amount for me, but what if all of the children of Stuyvesant Town claimed their money at the same moment. What would the bank do then?

At the Italian restaurant my father called "the spaghetti joint," Vic, the owner, worked all day by the front window, chopping clams for his sauce. He wore a once-white apron, stained as a butcher's. At dinner time he liked to come and sit with his regular customers, put his arm over the ladies' shoulders and tell jokes. He reeked of garlic. My father always winced when he saw him heading towards our table, but my mother tolerated him because she approved of his sauce, which was fresh and thick with clams. As we walked home to our apartment after dinner we'd blow on each other and laugh about our garlic breath.

China Boy, the Chinese restaurant—Mandarin, as they all were then—had a special "American menu" for children and grownups not daring enough for the exotic cuisine. We not only ordered the Chinese, but asked for chopsticks, which I had learned how to use from a Chinese friend. If you kneeled on your seat you could look over into the neighboring booth. I showed off with my chopsticks when another kid peered into our booth, dexterously entrapping a piece of green pepper slippery as an eel and popping it into my mouth.

There was a bar in the corner of China Boy, mysterious, with mirrors and glinting bottles and colored lights. My parents never ordered cocktails, but one time a waiter took pity on me and gave me one of the little paper parasols that went with the fancy drinks.

"Now you'll have to tip him extra," my mother whispered to my father. The umbrella's spokes were mere toothpicks, the pink paper delicate as flower petal. It did not survive being opened and shut more than twice, but I kept it for years.

Everyone in Stuyvesant Town owned a shopping cart. They still do. These were not the supermarket variety, four wheels with a child seat perched in front like a crow's nest on a ship. These were two-wheelers, that rolled when tilted, and rested upright on their wheels and two peg legs. They were designed to fold up flat, ideal for squeezing into the front closet in Stuyvesant Town apartments next to the umbrellas, narrow enough to be able to hook onto the supermarket cart in D'Agostino's. My mother's could hold two grocery bags in the bottom, two smaller ones perched on top, or two cloth laundry bags filled with clothes. Mothers with small children pushed the stroller with one hand and pulled the shopping cart with the other. To get into the elevator solo, they held the swinging door open with their rear end, maneuvered both stroller and cart around their bodies, and hopped inside the elevator just as the door shut.

Shopping carts were never strong enough to hold a child—though we tried, and inevitably bent out the bottom. They were well known to pinch fingers. They suffered the same mortality rate as umbrellas, and broken ones were often left by the incinerator door for the janitor to take away. The wheels, which would have been put to good use in a neighborhood where kids made soapbox cars or racers, were wasted on the children of Stuyvesant Town.

*At the piano with my mother—Albert Einstein
is perched on my hand, 1954*

IV

CREATURES

Stuyvesant Town children had acquaintance with few creatures aside from those they might see on forays to Central Park or the Bronx Zoo. The only other inhabitants of Stuyvesant Town beyond homo sapiens were brown English sparrows who congregated under the privet bushes and ants who colonized the cobblestone areas at the base of the buildings. Now there are legions of pigeons in Stuyvesant Town, and an abundance of squirrels—including some with black fur that would make a furrier lick his chops—but they were rare when I was growing up. It's hard to imagine how the squirrels ever discovered Stuyvesant Town. There was certainly not much habitat for them among the tenements and commercial buildings Stuyvesant Town replaced, nor in the years of construction. Word must have somehow gotten out to the populations at Washington Square Park and Herald Square from a few adventurous squirrels who had strayed beyond their usual turf.

When I grew up there were no mice, no rats, and no cockroaches in Stuyvesant Town. My parents had screens on their windows, but they were more to keep me from falling out than to keep insects from venturing in. There were few flying insects, not even mosquitoes or flies, and few spiders. Cobwebs were unheard of. The height of our windows may have been a determining factor, or the air pollution of the city. The only thing that came in through our windows was black soot from the nearby Consolidated Edison Company power plant, which we called by its nickname ConEd, to make it seem more benign. Our apartment was frequently dusted, but if I ever mistakenly leaned on the windowsill in the morning I'd have black smudges on the sleeves of my pajamas.

In the vast sterility of Stuyvesant Town an earthworm was an exotic, a butterfly a miracle. When we went to my grandfather's house in Mt. Kisco, forty miles north of the city, it wasn't just the woods and the landscape that was so different, but the population itself. In Mt. Kisco there were was an infinite number of insects—they flew, they crawled, they hopped. There were chipmunks and mice and moles and groundhogs and, miraculously, deer. There were toads and snakes. There were chickadees and robins and bluejays and crows and even hawks. Being a human was just one of a million possible things. In Stuyvesant Town it was easy to believe it was all.

Stuyvesant Town residents were forbidden to own pets beyond birds in cages and fish in tanks. Dogs, even visitors, were prohibited. A few people kept cats secretly in their apartments, but it was a risky business. One family we knew had a cat briefly, but it was reported to Stuyvesant Town authorities by their downstairs neighbors who claimed it disturbed them when it jumped from the bed to the carpeted floor. The cat was immediately removed. The threat "I'll report you," was always in the air in Stuyvesant Town. Any infraction, any misbehavior, any straying from the norm could result in the penalty all residents lived in fear of: eviction. Once cast out from this Eden you would never be allowed to return. There were other apartments in Manhattan (though few decent ones at a decent price) but there was no other Stuyvesant Town.

A visiting dog in Stuyvesant Town was a major event and quickly attracted a band of children. The owner would be as much of a celebrity as if she had a trained unicorn. Guards always arrived on the scene too soon, and the dog was led off. My friend Marla was afraid of dogs, even miniature ones. If she saw one she would scream "a dog! a dog!" as if she were reporting a dangerous beast, and run crying to her mother. Any report of a dog would send me flying to see the creature, and, if my luck was good, have a chance to pet it.

Occasionally stray dogs from the areas abutting Stuyvesant Town might wander in, get disoriented, and be unable to find their way out of the maze. Once they were reported, the ASPCA would come and cart them away.

One winter night, walking across the Oval, my father came across two stray dogs who looked lost and hungry. From my bedroom window I could spot them huddled near the fountain. I wanted to rescue the dogs, bring them upstairs, but my father assured me that come daylight, with some food in their bellies, they would find their way home. My mother filled two pie tins with food scraps and my father ventured out again in the cold to offer it to the dogs. When he came upstairs he reported that he had laid the food before one dog, but it hadn't begun to eat until it checked that its friend had been given something also.

I wept for those dogs, for their nobility, for the suffering of strays everywhere. This incident brought me to tears whenever I thought of it, as powerful as *Black Beauty*, a book that I hated and loved. I invoked it often—or perhaps it haunted me. That night marked, I guess, the end of my innocence. I understood then that the world was full of tragedies, and no one, even the most privileged child of Stuyvesant Town could insulate herself from them. There would always be lost, hungry dogs—not to mention starving children—and I couldn't rescue them all. I could never be perfectly happy.

I wanted a dog of my own. I wanted a dog intensely and consistently for my entire childhood. Instead I had to make do with the sort of pets children who live in apartments most often have: creatures smaller than a hand.

Eggbert, my salamander, had been captured in the brook in Mt. Kisco and brought back to Stuyvesant Town. After spending a number of years in an aquarium on the windowsill of the backroom, looking out over M playground, Twentieth Street, and the distant Empire State Building, he was laid to rest back in Mt. Kisco at the foot of a maple tree, with a small rock as headstone of his grave.

Eggbert swam and lolled in the algae-thick water in his tank, and basked on a floating piece of wood. Beef was his substitute for flies. I would take a tiny piece of chopped meat, roll it into a ball on the end of a length of black thread, then swing it over Eggbert's head. He would lunge in the air and strike, like a miniature dragon. The meat would come off in his mouth and I was able to jerk the string free. It was like fishing without a hook. He was a fat, utterly silent creature, and it was easy to conclude that he was contented, that he had no objection to his incarceration, to our having so arrogantly made his life a plaything of ours.

My parakeet, Albert Einstein, had free run of our apartment during the day and returned to his cage to eat and to sleep at night. He'd perch on the music rack on the piano while I practiced; sometimes rode on my hands while I did scales. He joined us at the dinner table. My mother discouraged him from walking across plates, but he'd strut around them, bending now and then to sample our food. He'd sit on the rim of a glass and reach down for drinks. I was always afraid he would fall in, which he did, only once. It was a long stemmed glass, with just a few drops of sherry in the bottom, and Albert Einstein, perhaps inebriated by the vapors of Harvey's Bristol Cream (my father's favorite) ended up upside down with his little bird head suctioned in the blue glass, and his bird claws scrambling wildly in the air. My mother grabbed glass in one hand and bird in the other and pulled them apart. There was a quick popping sound. My mother wiped Albert Einstein's head with a paper napkin and set him on his feet again. He staggered around the table until he recovered his equilibrium and his dignity, then he fluffed and preened. He kept a wary distance from stemware forever after.

In spite of his great intelligence and his weighty namesake, Albert Einstein was never able to master human speech. I did my best with books and a recording called "Teaching Your Parakeet How To Talk," but he stubbornly clung to his own language.

In his senior years Albert Einstein developed a growth around his beak, and my parents brought him to be examined at a city animal hospital. Unlike our apartment, the place had no screens. An incompetent vet let go of him, and he flew out the window. My parents ran through the streets calling for him, but had to come home with an empty cage. A few months later, my father spotted what might have been a blue parakeet among a flock of sparrows, in a neighborhood near where Albert Einstein had been lost. "He was bossing them all around," said my father. Whether or not it was story he had concocted for my benefit I never knew, but I chose to believe it. Albert Einstein, who had seen not one other bird for all the years of his life with us, now a leader among his own.

Roller skating with Barbara, 1954

V

GAMES

For all the years that I lived in Stuyvesant Town my father was engaged in a ongoing war of chess with our neighbor, Rab, who lived in 10H. The battles took place at unscheduled times, sometimes weekday evenings, sometimes Sunday afternoons, sometimes up in Rab's apartment, more often down in ours. They were indoors friends. They dropped by each other's houses, without coats, in any weather.

A former school principal, Rab was an administrator at the Board of Education. His real name was Irving, but I never heard anyone call him that. He had a deep voice used to authority, and exquisite grammar. When he rang our doorbell I'd call out, "Who's there" and he'd answer, "It is I." He looked like a bespectacled seal, with a tidy moustache and his thin, black hair slicked against his head.

They were an unlikely pair. My father was broad shouldered, athletic and gregarious. Rab was round shouldered, cerebral, and partial to irony. My father told jokes, collected from his patients and his lunch cronies, which were, in my mother's words "stupid and in poor taste." Rab posed verbal conundrums.

I'd hover around the sofa while they set up the chess board. "What's a sentence in English that has the word 'and' in it five time in a row?" Rab asked.

I puzzled over this one. My father gave up. My mother stepped out from the kitchen, as she often did, to lend her expertise. Finally we had to ask Rab to reveal the answer.

"A sign maker was instructing his assistant who was painting a sign for Lord and Taylor. There should be the same amount of space between Lord and and and and and Taylor."

I was impressed by this one and tried it out on all my friends. Never mind that the department store in question used an ampersand between its two names. It was unlikely that either Rab or his wife, Gertrude, would ever shop in that fashionable store.

When Rab's daughter grew up and moved out, her bedroom was turned into a study. It was there that I first discovered D. H. Lawrence's *Lady Chatterly's Lover*. It was set plainly on the shelf among Modern Library editions of contemporary literature. There was no doubt in my mind that Rab, an intellectual, had read every book by every great contemporary author, but there was also no doubt that he read them for nothing else but their literary merit. Only I, left to browse there while my father and Rab played chess in the living room, had any lascivious interest in the text.

My father and Rab played in relative silence and stillness for hours. At least it always seemed like hours. In our apartment they sat on the two wings of the sofa, leaning over the chessboard on the marble coffee table between them. My father smoked his pipe, which he called his "secret weapon." Rab stroked his moustache. My father, who liked activity and constant conversation, was a different personality, at a different tempo when he played chess. It was disquieting. It was as if he had been bewitched by chess, mesmerized by Rab. Chess was an exclusive game, a third person—especially a child—did not fit in, and it was a dull game to watch, especially since Rab and my father moved their pieces with inexorable lassitude.

When I was little I liked to play with my father's chess pieces, setting them up in noncombative royal families. All the pawns were princesses with stiff skirts. The lid of the wooden box that housed the chess pieces was the drawbridge to the castle. When I was older, my father showed me how to play chess and taught me some of his chess tricks—my favorite was sacrificing your queen to get to mate in five moves—but I was not temperamentally suited for the game. In part it was because I was impatient with strategies that involved meticulous long-range plotting, but more because I felt nervous the whole time I played. It was as if the chess people, which I had personified, were truly in jeopardy. Chess was a game that involved loss and elimination, symbolic death and destruction, unlike my favorite game Monopoly, which was based on acquisition, and the worst consequence was merely financial ruin.

My father and Rab kept a record of their combat on an index card stapled to the lid of the chess box. In all the years of playing, my father won exactly one third of the games. Either neither of them got any better at chess, or they both progressed at the same rate. My mother said that my father never actually beat Rab, it was only that when Rab was tired he occasionally made a mistake. But I think my father's triumphs came from his sometimes reckless style. Rab's strategy was always based on solid analysis. My father sometimes threw him off with an impulsive, unpredictable move.

Game after game, year after year, endless hours logged. My father and Rab, who had little else in common, were steady companions in struggle. Between them there was never any rancor, nor, it seemed, any real emotion about the game. They played to win, both of them, but the competitiveness never strayed beyond the world defined by the wooden figures on the board.

My father's other chess partner was Elliott, father of my friend Elaine, who lived uptown. We were perfectly matched families. While my father and Elliott played chess, my mother and Elaine's mother, Elsie, played Scrabble, and Elaine and I played Monopoly. On more than one occasion our parents got so involved in their games they forgot about our bedtimes. We'd get into pajamas and pretend to have fallen asleep in the bedroom, and our parents ended up letting us spend the night. For only children—which we both were—a sleepover date was a flirtation with siblinghood. Although in reality neither of us would have been happy to relinquish our only-child status, one of our favorite fantasy games was that we were sisters. When I slept over at Elaine's house, Elsie served us breakfast in bed, an indulgence granted at my house only when I was sick and in no condition to savor the luxury of it.

Children who grew up in small apartments depended on games that came in easy-to-store cardboard boxes for a large portion of their entertainment. Checkers and Chinese checkers and Parcheesi were standards then, and most kids I knew had Go To the Head of the Class and Sorry and, of course, Monopoly. The layouts of these boards were as familiar as our own apartments. For the duration of the game we'd lose ourselves in the settings—when we were little, the gooey fantasy of Candyland, later, the splendid but joyless mansion for Clue, the symmetrical city plan of Monopoly, where you progressed economically upward from the relative poverty of Mediterranean and Baltic Avenue to the grandeur of Park Place and Boardwalk. When the game was over we'd fold up the board and that world would disappear, and we'd be back in our room in Stuyvesant Town.

Outdoors, in Stuyvesant Town playgrounds, potsie and roly-poly were painted on the asphalt, as were two concentric circles, for circle games. Stuyvesant Town's recreation staff ran an active program for children, which included organized games, sports, and arts and crafts. Playground number 10, in front of my building, had no permanent equipment, and was the site of weekly programs, special events, and holiday parades and pageants.

There were thirteen children on my floor. None were exactly my age, but we played together, as kids in a small village do. We roamed among our apartments, sometimes joined by friends from other floors. We played balls and jacks and ran races in the hall and roller-skated on the exquisitely smooth rubber-tile floor. The standard ball was flesh-colored, sized for a child's palm. They were prized when new, but quickly acquired blemishes and dirt. We were forbidden to bounce them against the walls in the hall, where they purportedly would leave smudges, but various forms of handball were common when no grownups were around.

Two sisters lived in Apartment D. Marjorie was a few years older than I, Linda a few years younger. I settled for playing with Linda when no one older was available, but it was Marjorie who was the magnet.

One afternoon when I was disappointed to find both Marjorie and Linda were out, their mother invited me to play in their room anyway. The toys were on Linda's side of the room. Marjorie's side had a dressing table where she practiced to be a woman. I studied my face in her mirror, stroked her hairbrush, sniffed at her bottle of cologne. Marjorie had a foot-high glass jar that was filled with charms, the largest collection I had ever seen. Charms were plastic or metal miniatures, gum-machine prizes. They often had loops on top so that you could string them, but most of us kept them loose, to play with and trade. I inspected Marjorie's charms through the glass, and then I climbed up on a chair and dug one out. It was a tiny metal pitcher with a handle too small to get my pinky through and a spout that ended in a sharp point. Engraved on one side of it was something that might have been a flower. I set it upright on the dresser top. If Marjorie had been there she would certainly have given it to me had I asked for it, in fact she was such a generous person she would probably have offered it to me without my asking. But Marjorie was not there. I heard her mother coming down the hall. I picked up the charm to put it back, but afraid to be caught up on a chair, handling the jar, I slipped it into the cuff of my sock. I wore white anklets that were stretchy nylon, and the elastic kept the charm snug against my inside ankle bone.

It was the first and only thing I have ever stolen in my life. If Marjorie ever noticed it missing she never said so; certainly I was never suspected of removing it, though I waited daily to be accused. I planned to sneak back into Marjorie's room and replace it in the jar, but the perfect opportunity never arose. The charm made me hate myself. Marjorie was as kind to me as ever before, and I felt like a traitor to her, and to her entire family. I did not know that I was a person who could steal; the very idea of it had once been unimaginable. I wondered who I was, how I had known myself so poorly. I wondered what else I was capable of. And I wondered about everyone else. If I was a thief, then what about all those other little girls, who, from the outside looked as innocent, as honest as I did? Was it possible that they were thieves, too?

I could not return the charm to the jar for fear of getting caught doing so. I could not throw it away, because it was, I thought, too valuable. I could not play with it because I could not let anyone see it, nor could I enjoy playing with it. So I kept it in my drawer, among the purses and costume jewelry and embroidered, unused handker-chiefs, hidden and re-hidden in new spots, and always it reminded me of the darker self I didn't know I had.

VI

NIGHT

When I awoke in the middle of the night as a child, our apartment was as quiet as if we were isolated in a dense forest. It seemed that people were asleep all around me—in the apartment above, below, on three sides, in all the apartments in the building and the adjoining building and the look-alike buildings across the street—and I was the only one awake. The silence of Stuyvesant Town was so great it was as if a spell had been laid on the place, and I, alone, had escaped. I thought of a fairytale where the cook fell asleep over her pastry dough, and the servant boy fell asleep as he ran to fetch the shallots from the gardener and the cat fell asleep as she lifted her paw to lick, and the minstrel fell asleep with a chord only half strummed on his lute—all of them awaiting the prince who would break through the magic. No prince ever came to Stuyvesant Town, only the sunrise. Even if it was a gloomy morning (and I could hear the tugboats on the river calling out their warnings in the fog), the sunrise invisible, it still recalled people from their slumbers.

There was a nightlight in my room and another in the bathroom and a dark hall to negotiate between them. Long after I was done using the toilet, I would still sit there and stare at the floor tiles—olive green turned grey by night—and the fringe of the bathmat, like miniature ponytails gathered all around, and press against the cold porcelain of the sink beside me. The night seemed long as a lifetime.

It was then, in that most alone time that I ever was, for children are rarely totally alone the way grownups might be, that I thought about my being, and my mortality. I did not use those words or know those concepts then. What I felt was a terror that I would die, that I would cease to exist, and a bewilderment about what my very existence meant.

How could I not be? And yet, what about the time that was before I existed, a period of time that was documented in the lives of my parents and my grandparents before them. There was the wedding picture of my parents, the two people who loved me most, and yet at the time of that photograph, there was no wisp of me. Where was I then?

The terrible conclusion was that if I had not existed before I was born, then surely I would not exist after I was dead. I would be as nothing as I had once been. The thought of my death would make me weep. I would miss myself! I would miss being alive!

Perhaps all children wonder about what it is to be alive, worry about what it will be like to be dead. I suspect that most never talk about it with their parents. Certainly they do not talk about it among themselves. For one, they lack the vocabulary. But what really halts them is the power and terror of it. I believed it to be mine, alone. It was my closely held secret. There were no clues that other children might feel it, no feelers from them that they might want to speak of it. We talked about death, of course, but it was all joking. We scared each other and ourselves with ghost stories that involved worms wriggling out through a corpse's eye sockets, and passed on all sorts of misinformation about death, burial, and cremation. But we never confessed our true fears. We never told each other about waking up in the middle of the night and wondering what our existence meant, wondering what life was.

I had a fantasy that I was the star of a play that was my life. I acted my part spontaneously—I simply was—while everyone around me was an actor who was working from a script, which was my fate. My parents, the most talented actors, had the most consuming parts.

Everyone whom I knew was a actor, too; the people I passed on the street were bit players. Sometimes the same extras might be used in crowd scenes, but only so I wouldn't notice. I believed that I couldn't let on that I had penetrated the secret, that doing so might jeopardize all those actors, including people whom I loved, since their mission was not only to play their parts, but play them so convincingly I would never guess the truth.

Certainly each person is aware that he or she is the only one looking out, while everyone else is in the same outside dimension. I know that others have had a fantasy similar to mine as children. Like mortality, it's something else that children never speak of with each other.

Occasionally when I got up in the middle of the night I would run into my father who was up, walking off a nightmare. His nightmares were about World War II, which he called simply "The War," as if there hadn't been or wouldn't be any others. As a dentist in a unit of MPs, my father was spared actual combat, but he had witnessed fighting and its aftermath, and had often enough been afraid for his life. His nightmares were replays of certain scenes he struggled to forget. During daytime, my father's tales about the war were primarily about other soldiers and the civilian friends he made. His anecdotes, even when they were based on a horror of war, always had a humorous cast. My father made his experiences in Normandy sound like a kids' camping trip—digging a foxhole, and rigging up a tarpaulin to keep out the rain. The word "foxhole" made his shelter sound like a cozy den, and made my city-born and bred father seem like an innocent, wild creature. When he related his experience about being chased by a buzz bomb while riding in a jeep, it had a cartoon quality to it. I pictured my father telling his trusty corporal to drive like hell, while he looked back at the bomb coming after them, a bomb as big and ludicrous as floats in the Macy's Thanksgiving Day parade. My father's exploits in the mayhem of war always seemed to have as a soundtrack music from the Keystone Cops. The fact he had made it home alive and uninjured was the proof that tamed these tales, that made it possible for us to laugh about them.

But at night the hiss of the buzz bomb roused my father from his nightmare, and he walked the hallway of our apartment, shaking it away, shaking away his memories of the dead, of the faces of people in the concentration camp when they were freed, of buildings collapsing in smoke and fire. He never told me specifically about these things at night, but I knew about them. I had seen photographs in books and magazines. And I knew that the comic buzz bomb of day had come unleashed from its tethers and was chasing my father for real now in dream after dream.

I believed my father was a hero. He had liberated the Jews from the concentration camps. He had destroyed Hitler. All his activities had been on the side of The Good. He was not suffering guilt. His nightmares were as innocent as my own—good was pursued by evil, there was no ambiguity.

I'd walk with him along the long hallway, the cool apartment walls close beside our shoulders, the grey wall-to-wall carpeting warm beneath our bare feet.

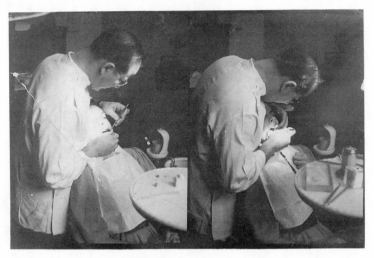

My father with a dental patient

VII

DENTISTRY

My father, a dentist, often talked about his work at the dinner table. Complicated questions of bridges and weak teeth would be illustrated by moving around cups and cutlery. My half-drunk glass of milk would be a molar, a fork would be a bridge, a cup of coffee would be an impacted wisdom tooth. My father would describe his treatments and plans, and my mother, whether asked for it or not, would offer advice. Sometimes this was taken with good-humored respect and my father would wink and say to me "your mother's a smart woman." Sometimes a heated argument ensued, and my father would end up shouting that my mother didn't know what she was talking about, and she should have gone to dental school herself.

"I probably should have," my mother would say. It was medical school that she had longed to go to, but felt she couldn't afford, so she had settled for a master's degree in zoology from Columbia, instead.

My father had endless compassion for true suffering, but little patience for people who complained "about nothing." If people turned out to be what he called pains in the neck, he gave them their money back and told them to find another dentist. My mother thought he was a terrible business man, and was constantly trying to reform him. She knew, however, that though his practice might flourish if she took charge of his office, their marriage would never survive.

My father took care of anyone who came to him, whether they could pay or not, including the kind of down-and-out souls my mother would not choose to sit next to in a waiting room. My father hated paperwork and sometimes did work gratis rather than be bothered with the forms required by Medicaid, Medicare, or insurance plans. My mother urged my father to work longer hours—Saturdays maybe and some evenings, and to step up the pace of his practice. My father refused. He didn't like the pressure of patients in the waiting room, and although he had two fully equipped operating rooms, he didn't like running between patients in two chairs. He liked to sleep till eight in the morning and he liked to have lunch with the men he called his "cronies," Greek furriers, who met in a Greek restaurant and told each other jokes that their wives disapproved of. Dentists are not known for their longevity. At his fiftieth Tufts Dental School reunion my father was one of the few still alive, and my mother conceded that he may have been right about his work schedule all along.

My father saved teeth with the zeal of a priest saving souls. His greatest triumph was when he could save the teeth of someone who had been told by another dentist they had to all come out. He was always interested in developing new techniques and streamlining old ones. With my mother's prodding he published some of his ideas in *Dental Digest*, a magazine that too often lay about on our coffee table with its full-color photographs of details of dental surgery. My father was a pioneer in tooth implants, and gloried in a particular young Greek furrier, whose teeth were a mess from poor diet but who had great jawbones intact—a perfect human subject.

My father was a devotee of Rube Goldberg, and my mother constantly had to guard our home against his inventiveness. My favorite invention of his—which never got beyond the paper design stage—was a baby carriage that had wheels on springs that dropped when they came to a curb (there were no curb cuts in those days for wheelchairs) and lowered the carriage gently, so the baby would not slide to the top and bang its head. (In his cartoon drawing of an old-style carriage, five-pointed stars explode from the baby's head.)

In his office, my father had free rein. Little cotton balls were applied to the wire pulleys of his dental drill to look like bunnies endlessly chasing each other. The swinging door of his operating room he had painted (without consulting with my mother) a bright yellow, for "all the cowards who walk through." My father hated the thought of anyone having suffered at the hands of a dentist, of anyone being afraid of dentists. He saw his job as not simply to restore people's teeth, but to restore their faith.

Patients were encouraged to call my father at home when they were in dental trouble. In emergencies, he'd meet a patient at his office off-hours, using my mother to fill in for his nurse, a task she rose to with professional éclat, though the risk was great that she would second-guess him about his procedures when they got home. More than once this happened on Christmas morning. Grateful patients brought my father bottles of whiskey (five-star Metaxas, if they were Greeks), home-baked desserts, and offered us wholesale discounts at their businesses. A dozen of my father's patients were furriers and my mother could have had a mink coat at cost from any of them. It was a constant, nearly comic, dilemma of her life that although she lusted after a mink coat, she could never actually bring herself to buy one. She and I were given mink earmuffs as a consolation prize. Though the sight of a dead animal would give me nightmares as a child, in those days I hadn't any qualms about wearing their pelts.

At Christmas my mother had my father send out cards to all his patients—sedate cards that said Seasons Greetings (in respect to his Jewish patients) with his name engraved inside. He received dozens of cards from patients and former patients. "Merry Christmas, Happy New Year! The dentures are great!" "Joyous Noel! That crown doesn't give me trouble any more."

Not everyone liked my father's manner, for sure. Or his office, or, perhaps, his dentistry. My parents had a few good friends who didn't use my father as their dentist, and the subject was always a sore one. The most outrageous case was the friend who always complained about his dentist and asked my father's advice informally, but never went to him as a patient. Another friend had been treated by my father regularly, then abruptly switched dentists. The reason was mysterious but aroused endless speculation. My mother was sure it was something my father said—he was, undeniably, impatient and frank—my father was hurt and baffled. Few patients complained about my father's prices or found they could get things done better, cheaper elsewhere, and I can't imagine that anyone ever doubted his honesty. My father knew dentists who put in fillings that weren't really necessary, who always found some work to do in any billable mouth that was presented to them, and it made him furious.

My father got referrals from a network of friends and family. A mainstay of his practice were Greek furriers and florists, who worked near his office. Sometimes he picked up patients in unlikely ways. One time he was ticketed for throwing "household refuse" into the litter box on his corner. The police had traced him through his name and address on discarded envelopes. The cop who went up to my father's office to deliver the summons ended up complaining about some problem, getting advice and became a devoted patient. The same was true about the state trooper who pulled my father over for speeding on the Saw Mill River Parkway. When my father got out of the car and went back to talk to the cop I was terrified he was going to be shot. When I dared to peep up over the back seat I saw my father and the cop laughing by the side of the police car. My father's excuse for speeding was that he had been distracted by my mother's nagging. The cop empathized. The next time I looked back, the state trooper was holding his mouth open and pointing to a troublesome molar.

The first dental office my father had when I was a child was in the St. Moritz Hotel, with a view of Central Park. It had the advantage of proximity to Rumpelmeyer's, New York's fanciest ice-cream emporium, but business was slow. My father fared much better when he moved to a little building on the corner of Eighth Avenue and Twenty-seventh Street, close to the flower, fur, and garment district. There was a small grocery store on the first floor. My father's office and a commercial artist's studio were on the second. They shared a bathroom in the hall, an old-fashioned water closet with a pull chain and a wooden seat. The artist created window displays for Tiffany's, and the jewels were so well insured that he was able to bring them to his studio and fashion the scenery and props to show them off. I saw them there and touched them—in that rough studio, surrounded by wood and cardboard, paint and scraps—and then saw them in Tiffany's windows, properly enthroned, behind thick glass.

Subsequent tenants, after the artist moved, were not as desirable. The worst point came when a family (my mother called them gypsies) occupied the space illegally and sent their beautiful, grey-eyed children out to beg. Patients of my fathers, mounting the stairs to his office, would be distracted from their dental woes by plaintive appeals for quarters. The family mysteriously disappeared every time the landlord came to investigate. These children fascinated me. They whisked in and out of the building with elfin speed, whispered in a strange language, and regarded me with suspicious disdain. One day the whole family vanished and left behind not a single trace of their occupancy.

One night a thief broke into my father's office by climbing through the skylight. My father's gold was well hidden in the laboratory drain, so the thief had to be content with a few dental tools. My father was alone in his office for the next robbery. His nurse had just gone out for lunch, when a man with a sawed-off shotgun burst in. He was after drugs and syringes. Sitting in his revolving green Naugahyde desk chair with his hands in the air, my father calmly told him to help himself.

"That doesn't even look like a real gun you've got there," my father said, while the thief was rifling through his desk.

At this point of the narration, whenever my father told the story (which he did often), my mother always moaned "Oh, Nick you could have been killed!"

The thief glowered at my father. "Wanna bet?" He cocked the gun and was about to pump some holes in the floor beside the desk. "All, right, all right, I believe you!" my father said, "I don't want any holes in my new linoleum."

When I was in high school my father moved to a better location, a block south of Penn Station. His office was on the second floor, just above the entrance, and it was a thrill to see the sign *Dr. Nicholas C. Demas, Dental Surgeon,* black letters on a white plastic background, hanging in the windows that overlooked Seventh Avenue as I rode by in the bus. To protect my father from holdups, the waiting room in the new office was kept separate from the interior offices by a locked door that was opened by a buzzer. But the system failed twice.

One day, late in the afternoon, a man in a leather jacket came into the waiting room and told the nurse that he had a terrible toothache. He gave his name as David Brown, and said he was a new patient. He was big as a professional football player. When my father tells the story he says "he was a big, black man." When I call him on that, he insists it's not a racist comment, just a way to describe someone. When I point out to him that he never described the other robber as white, he's puzzled. In my father's world, in the Stuyvesant Town world I grew up in, everyone was assumed to be white, and you mentioned skin color only if they weren't.

My father was always a softy for someone in pain. He asked permission of the patient in the chair and one patient in the waiting room, and slipped this David Brown into his second operating room. My mother, who was picking my father up after work, was waiting in the extra room beside the office, which had a door to the outside hall.

My father examined David Brown's tooth, took an X-ray, but couldn't find anything wrong. Just as they were walking back out through the office, David Brown said, just loud enough for my father to hear, "This is a stickup," and pulled a gun.

Perhaps it was his anger at being duped this way that gave my father rare strength for a sixty-seven year old. He lunged at David Brown, held his hand down and wrestled him back through the doorway into the waiting room. The patient in the waiting room, a Greek furrier, looked up from *Reader's Digest.*

"Grab him," my father shouted in Greek, and the furrier leaped up and got hold of David Brown from the back. My father, who hadn't used his fists since college boxing team days delivered what he described as "a brilliant left hook." The gun dropped to the floor. In the meantime the nurse alerted my mother, who ran out the back door and down to the lobby where she got someone to call the police.

David Brown sank his teeth into the furrier's hand till he let go, broke away and escaped out the door. The police arrived within minutes, but too late to catch Mr. Brown, and he was quickly lost in the crowds near Penn Station.

"Hell, you didn't need our help," said the cops to my father. They took the gun for evidence, as well as the leather jacket, which David Brown had left on a chair in the waiting room. My father got to keep the X-ray, which he has to this day. The envelope is marked "Bandit" with David Brown's name followed by a question mark. "I'm sure he made the name up on the spot," says my father. He holds the X-ray up to the light for me. "He was a young man," he says, "his wisdom teeth hadn't come down yet." He points at the tooth in question. " See," he says, "I was right. There was nothing wrong with that molar."

My father was alone in his office when he was held up the last time. Once again, the thief pretended he had a dental emergency, and my father took him in. This time he didn't waste an X-ray. The thief jumped him from behind and caught him in a headlock. They wrestled on the floor and it might have been an even match, except the door opened and the thief's partner came to his rescue.

"Okay guys," said my father, loosening his grip. "You win. I can't take on two of you at once."

These thieves were disappointed to find more checks than cash in my father's desk. They took his wallet, but were persuaded by him to give him back all his cards and papers. They also left him change for his carfare home, as he requested. He couldn't persuade them not to tie him up, but when they went to gag him with a dirty towel he told them where the clean linen was kept and they fetched one instead.

"You know fellows," said my father, just before the gag was stuffed in his mouth, "this is a hell of a way to make a living."

"Oh, but I'm going to night school," one of the thieves said. My father always chuckled over this line.

It didn't take my father too long after the thieves were gone to get himself untied and ungagged. He called the police, then he called his dental technician, whom he was supposed to have called earlier, to check on a set of dentures.

At this point in the story my father always paused. The entire episode seemed to have been created for his great punchline. "I called up my man Tommy," he said, "and told him I was sorry I hadn't called him earlier, but I was all tied up."

My mother never smiled at this story. Later that afternoon, the police informed my parents that the same pair hit another dental office a few blocks away, and during the robbery the dentist died of a heart attack.

My father was seventy-three when my mother finally succeeded in persuading him to retire.

VIII

MUSIC

Pianos were so common in Stuyvesant Town apartments, they seemed like basic appliances. Once a family acquired a piano it remained a permanent fixture, even when a rebellious daughter quit taking lessons, at least until the children grew up and left home. Our piano was a Baldwin Acrosonic spinet—a stunted version of an upright. It had "blond" wood, ash probably, and the plain, squat look that in the fifties was called "modern." Some neighbors had similar instruments housed in different style cases—mahogany or cherry, some had old-fashioned uprights with ivory keys, yellowed and chipped as old teeth. Ours came with a piano bench, but others had round piano stools that spun to an infinite variety of heights, the best with feet carved to resemble the claws of pterodactyls.

A few families had grand pianos—baby grands, that is. Since they did not fit into the elevator, the only way to get a grand into a Stuyvesant Town apartment was through the living room window. The piano had to submit to the indignity of being hauled up outside the building by ropes from the roof; the entire window had to be removed from its frame, then welded back into place. But getting a grand piano into a Stuyvesant Town living room was only the start of the trouble. It took up a good quarter of the area, blocking either the window or the path between dining area and hall. It looked as out of proportion as a cow in a dog house, and that was before you lifted the lid. (A rare occurrence: the surface area of grand pianos was most often used as display space for framed photographs and for piles of books and papers. One family we knew put their Christmas tree up there.)

The purchase of a grand piano, for some neighbors, occurred with a corresponding increase in their own prosperity and their child's musical virtuosity, but it was more usual that tenants had owned them before moving to Stuyvesant Town, or inherited them after they'd moved in. They were artifacts of spacious, prewar New York apartments, relics of another life. A grand piano was a status symbol of a special sort, for it spoke not only of wealth, but of a family's cultural priorities. It took up such a large percentage of the small amount of a Stuyvesant Town apartment's living space, you had to be vain, or mad, to have one.

In an apartment in the attached building, two floors below us and diagonally across from our backroom, there was an older girl who played the piano. She would play for hours without getting up, the most difficult sonatas and preludes and études. When I saw her out on the street, she was fat and homely, and had the look of someone resigned to that, but she played the piano with such exquisite passion we would stand by the window to hear her play. My father would turn off the television, my mother would come from the kitchen, dishtowel in hand, and I would leave my homework half-done. We'd open the window and turn off the light and lean on the windowsill and listen to her. She never noticed us. From our angle we could see part of the grand piano, the side of her head, sometimes her hands moving on the keyboard. We never saw anyone else in the apartment, and perhaps we were the only people who ever listened to her. We never knew her name.

Some Stuyvesant Town children had piano teachers who came to their apartment, like doctors who made house calls. Others went to their teacher's home, or to music schools. Third Street Music School had been a discovery of one Stuyvesant Town mother, and quickly word spread. A Settlement House, Third Street had been established in 1894 to provide music lessons for the indigent children of Manhattan's Lower East Side. But they did not turn away anyone, no matter how prosperous. Lessons were subsidized, and even for families not considered "needy" the cost was considerably lower than if you studied with that same teacher privately. The school is now on Eleventh Street (though its name hasn't changed); the original building was on Third Street, between First and Second Avenue.

It was a neighborhood as different from Stuyvesant Town as I could imagine. Old ladies draped blankets over their windowsills and leaned out of their tenement to gossip with their neighbors. They had fat little dogs with legs barely thick enough to hold their bodies up, dogs that lifted their legs on the garbage cans that lined the street, on the wrought iron fence along the front of Third Street Music School. Around the corner, on Second Avenue, was a Yiddish Theater and Metro Music Store, where we went to buy music books, or, what seemed infinitely more grown up, sheet music for an individual piece. Bums from the Bowery lined up outside the blood bank to sell the only thing they had left of value. They were given oranges when they left, which they held out to us, as we ran past them from the bus stop to the shelter of Third Street Music School. "Hey, little kid," they'd call, "have an orange! Hey, little kid!"

When you entered the front door, half a flight up took you to the grand rooms: auditorium, library, director's office; half a flight down took you to the window-less waiting room, and the cashier's lines, like betting windows at a race track, where you paid for your lessons.

Miss Coffin sat at her desk in the front hall, directing newcomers, admonishing children who ran, and keeping guard against inebriated gentlemen who wandered into the building by mistake. She was an ancient person, no taller than a child, with aristocratic posture and voice. She wore gold-rimmed glasses, black crepe dresses, and lace-up high-heeled shoes that might have been in style a century before. Her name seemed ridiculously appropriate, but her family, we were told, was illustrious. Her Coffin ancestors, reportedly, made caskets, and their business was so successful their brand name became used, generically, for all caskets. However, when I check out "coffin" in the dictionary now, the story is discredited. The word's origin is Middle English, "cofin," meaning basket. I have no way to verify the other story: that she was the daughter of the family who had donated one of the three attached brownstones that made up the settlement house building, that she had known it when the library had been their private collection, when the director's office—with its black grand piano so shiny I could see my reflection in it and its Persian rug—was their salon, when the spacious bedrooms hadn't been divided up into tiny lesson rooms, no two alike.

When a bum straggled into the lobby of the music school, Miss Coffin stood up at her desk.

"I'm sorry sir, but you'll have to leave," she said, her voice high and clear.

"Please, ma'am, all I want is a drink of water."

A plea for water could not be denied. Miss Coffin escorted the man to the water fountain, waited beside him while he bent to drink, and escorted him promptly out again.

It was hard to imagine how all the pianos got into the lesson rooms upstairs. There was no elevator, and the hallways were narrow, the windows narrow, too. It was hard to imagine how the floors supported the weight of so many pianos. Some of the rooms were no wider than closets. The hallways were filled with a cacophony of sonatas and scales.

I started with piano lessons, but it was violin lessons I really wanted, and after a few years my parents let me take violin lessons, too. It wasn't the sound of a violin that attracted me, it was the appeal of an instrument that was just that, an instrument, as opposed to the piano, which seemed more like a piece of furniture. There was a lot of paraphernalia that went with a violin: a shoulder pad, a pitch pipe, a bow, a little cake of glistening rosin. You had to tune up. You had to rosin your bow. You had to create the notes. At the piano you simply pushed down keys. I loved the violin, the way the wood curved and the grain rippled in the light, the S holes that let me peer into the secret depths. We rented my first instrument from the school. The printed label inside said Antonius Stradivarius, Cremona, the words "copy of" so tiny that they were almost invisible. Perhaps my violin was a real one. I loved to carry the violin case as I walked through Stuyvesant Town, arousing the envy of all those children who played nothing more interesting than the piano.

As soon as I was able to draw a bow across the four strings without screeching, I was drafted for the Third Street Music School Junior Orchestra. There, in the back ranks of the third violin section, my little sounds joined with the large, magnificent voice. At the end of the year I got to be part of the annual Town Hall concert. No matter that the audience was filled with parents and patrons of the music school, no matter that my contribution to Purcell was predominately a lot of open-string Gs and Ds.

Third Street Music school had its battalion of ordinary music students, like me, and it had its stars. The stars were not so much better simply because they practiced; they were different from the rest of us. They were the ones who went last at the school recitals, whose virtuosity we all took a proprietorial interest in. They had vibratos, they played in fifth and sixth position, harmonics, notes too high to hear, and their bows moved as if they were alive, and the hand holding them was just along for the ride. Some of them would go on to conservatories—Juilliard or Mannes School of Music. What I didn't know then was that they were already too old to be prodigies, and few, if any, of them, would have that rare combination of luck, stamina, and genius to become famous on the concert stage when they grew up.

In addition to my violin and piano lessons at Third Street, I took classes in music theory. Music was just sounds, yet in theory we learned there was an underlying system—majors and their melancholy relative minors—that organized it all. It was magical that the order of sharps in key signatures, FCGDAEB, was exactly opposite the order of flats, BEADGCF. And it was magical the way the key of a piece was revealed in the key signature, half a step from the last sharp, or the next to the last flat. It was as if someone had designed all this to make it easier for kids to memorize. But no one had, it had just happened that way. Like a math trick, like the nine times table where the two digits of every multiple of nine added up to equal nine itself.

When I was around eleven, our theory class moved on to musical composition. The instructor was a young composer, whose face was pitted with acne scars. He was so poor he wore the same moth-ravaged sweater week after week. Every time we passed a piano we were to hum "A" above middle "C," and then check ourselves. Sometimes this worked, and sometimes it didn't. He believed that if we could capture a perfect "A" we could find intervals above or below it and so sing any note we wanted. He was convinced this was possible even for a child like me, not blessed with perfect pitch.

One night I awoke in the desolate hours before morning with a tune forming in my head. I got out of bed and stood by the window. The Oval was hushed and still. I was the only one awake in all of Stuyvesant Town. I hummed the tune, and it spun effortlessly from me. It was so beautiful my eyes pricked with tears. From the dark living room I retrieved my spiral music notebook and a pencil. I didn't want to turn on the lights and break the spell. I got back into bed and by the light of my nightlight started writing out the tune on the blank staff, humming parts of it over and over again till I could figure out the notes. I scribbled furiously, afraid I would lose the melody before I could get it all down on paper. This, then, was what it was like to be a composer. This was what Mozart and Beethoven felt like. I didn't bother with a key signature or a time signature, I just wrote out the notes in a long, measureless string, trying to capture the rhythm as best I could. When I was done, I laid the notebook beside my bed and snuggled back down under the covers, the melody warm in my head. I would bring my composition to my teacher. I'd amaze him. I'd amaze my class. I would amaze the world.

In the morning when I awoke and saw the notebook, the thrill of the night's creation came back to me. I couldn't remember the tune at first, only that it had been beautiful. I ran to the living room and sat at the piano. It was hard to decipher my handwriting. Note by note I started to pick at the melody. Then, after a line, it all came back to me. And as soon as it did, I was immediately devastated. For the tune was a song I recognized; it was not something I had made up at all. What I had written out in the middle of the night, believing I had composed it, was the Christmas carol, "O Holy Night," written in the 1800s by the French composer Adolph Adam.

That was the only time in my life when I had an exultation of music composition. Perhaps the chagrin of discovering I was a mere plagiarist was worth the price of that short-lived thrill, those heady hours when I believed myself to be a real composer, someone far more talented than I really was, or ever would be.

For the final project for our theory class we had to set a poem to music. I chose Emerson's "Concord Hymn," ("By the rude bridge that arched the flood . . . "). I have it still, in that same spiral music notebook. It is a quotidian creation, an uninspiring melody and some predictable chord accompaniment for the piano part. Still, to some ears, no doubt, it sounded more musical than the original composition our teacher played for us at the end of the year, a piece of "modern music" with great clumps of dissonant chords and nothing that seemed organized, or made sense, or was predictable, the way I had come to expect music to be.

Taking piano and violin lessons changed the contour of my week. It inched along in the days following my lessons, and then moved with catastrophic speed to the day of the next lessons, for which I was invariably poorly prepared. Like most normal children, I hated to practice. At the end of every lesson I would be resolute with good intentions to practice as diligently as my teachers hoped, yet I encountered perfectly legitimate excuses to avoid practicing day after day. I practiced when my mother's nagging reached a crescendo, when she threatened to stop my lessons and sell the piano and violin. (I always retorted "fine with me!" though I never meant that, secure that she had not meant it either.) When I did sit down to practice, I spent more time picking my way through new music than working on my assigned pieces. Repetition was like reading the same paragraph in a book over and over again when I wanted to read ahead.

In Stuyvesant Town, practicing was public business. I could hear Randy at the spinet a floor below me practicing Schumann's "Wild Horseman," while I hadn't progressed beyond "First Loss." And if the competition was not enough, there were my friends Elaine and Carol Jean, whose mothers and mine compared our progress (and had us play for each other) fostering a climate that would make any child psychologist cringe. It was certainly a lapse in my mother's otherwise enlightened child-rearing techniques, but I believe that even the wisest of parents can be contaminated by the fever of competition on their children's behalf and embark on a venture that wisdom would lead them to realize would be counterproductive.

I honed my sight-reading skills, to the extent that I was sometimes able to fool a teacher into thinking I had practiced a piece that actually I was playing for the first time. This was harder to get away with on the violin, since fingering and bowing techniques required a certain amount of physical practice. I had a succession of violin teachers. Mr. Grossman, who made his living playing violin in the orchestra pits of Broadway shows, lost patience with me early on and my lessons were clearly as unpleasant for him as they were for me. Mostly I was a perpetual disappointment to kinder, younger teachers, gentle women who had once been "stars" in their young days and who now made marginal livings teaching music.

The piano teacher whom I studied with longest was Palma Szirmai. She had soft, plump arms and fine, elegant fingers. She had fled from Poland just before the war and seen great tragedy, though she never spoke of it. She loved Chopin and Paderewski, and when I was particularly unprepared I could easily divert her from listening to my exercises to playing new pieces she was going to assign me.

I somehow escaped having to perform violin solos at the music school's recitals, but piano recitals were a perennial torture. All our performance pieces were arranged in a hierarchy of difficulty, and we awaited our trials on the front row of folding chairs in the auditorium. The metal was cold against my bare legs, and my hands were remarkably both frozen and coated with sweat. One by one we took our turn, climbing up the stairs at the side of the stage, disappearing for a minute behind the gathered curtains, then walking out across the stage, blinking in the light. White marble busts of great musicians, sentinels along the sides of the auditorium, gazed at us with pupil-less eyes. Certainly they never imagined the terror their compositions would inspire.

There is no logical reason for stage fright. You are in no actual danger, you suffer no physical pain. The audience is on your side, wishing you well, and will remain polite and encouraging through wrong notes, forgotten repeats, aborted trills. They will applaud even the most wretched performance. Yet logic never prevailed. The piece that I could perform perfectly by heart at my own piano became an enigma on stage. The piano, which responded sympathetically to my touch when no one was in the auditorium, rebelled under my fingers when an audience was present. Even my own hands were afflicted, the joints went stiff, the finger pads felt numb. My mind, as if I were drugged, could not remember anything at all, and although my fingers could recreate the pattern of movements I had drilled them in, they had no traction on the slick keyboard.

I survived, I know, most concerts with only minor mistakes and a tendency to play with accelerated speed, perhaps in an effort to shorten my ordeal. The concert that ended my career, though, was the one that seems to affect my memory of all the others. I was play-ing a Chopin waltz, a waltz I knew as well as I have ever known a piece of music. Half way through, like an ice skater in competition who catches a toe on a rough spot of ice, I lost my footing, and when I re-traced my steps to correct it, I couldn't pick up where I had been. I had no choice but to go to the beginning of the piece and start all over. My anxiety about that one spot made me stumble again when I reached it, and again I balked and could not get past it, and had to start over from the beginning. I don't know how many times I cir-cled in that loop. In my memory it goes on and on. But that, of course, is the way memory seizes and distorts events. I think it is likely that after a few attempts I abandoned that section of the piece and moved ahead to the final movement. But that part is lost to me. What I remember is running off the stage without bowing, hearing the ritual applause, and escaping out the back of the auditorium, out the front door of the building, to the open sky of Third Street.

In spite of my desperate dénouement, in the car on the way home, my parents gave me the present they had brought for me. It was a gold charm for my bracelet, a miniature grand piano with three semiprecious stones imbedded on the lid, which opened with hinges too tiny to see. I cried all the way home, for my humiliation, for the disappointment I had given my piano teacher, for the shame I had brought upon my parents, and because I did not deserve the gift they had given me. I'm sure it never occurred to them that that gold charm would cause me such wretchedness, but my mother did not press me when I said I didn't want it hung on my charm bracelet, and I kept it unworn all these years, tucked in a corner of my jewelry box.

At home, in the safety of our Stuyvesant Town living room, when no one was listening, I played the Chopin waltz. My fingers moved firmly and smoothly over the keys, and the place where I had stumbled was sealed over like a perfectly healed wound.

IX

SCHOOL

Children at Hunter College Elementary School were not called smart, but rather "intellectually gifted." It was a label we were all able to pronounce with precision at age six, though we were not able to spell it correctly, some of us for many years, if at all. Spelling was not a skill that Hunter emphasized, along with other things, like borrowing when you did subtraction. We were left to figure out for ourselves the more routine manipulations of math, and as for reading, that was a skill we were expected to have acquired before we entered school. I was six when I started Hunter and was put in second grade. We were all a grade ahead of ourselves.

We were called the Model School, which meant that Hunter College students and professors often sat in the back of our classroom observing us, and we were the guinea pigs for new educational ideas. For the most part we got used to being studied, but I was occasionally aware of someone watching me and taking notes, and felt like a performer—a child, impersonating an intellectually gifted child. I wonder what they gleaned from us that was applicable to students at large.

Supposedly, we all had high IQs (150+ was the median) though none of us seemed like geniuses. One girl, reported to have an IQ over 170, was the problem child of the class, as if IQ were like temperature and hers had passed into the fever zone. In a fit of temper once—no uncommon thing—she mashed gooey chewing gum against her head and had to have chunks of hair cut off to remove it. We would stand around and watch her tantrums with curious detachment. She had white skin that flushed red quickly, and when she lay on the floor screaming and kicking, her skirt lifted up, displaying her red thighs and her white panties.

To compete for Hunter you had to take what was called an intelligence test. In the waiting room anxious mothers with children secured between their knees awaited their darling's turn. My examiner strung colored beads on a string, then pulled them off and asked me to restring them in the same order. There was no pattern to the beads, but I could picture the sequence. Certainly this aspect of the test favored girls. I was shown big ink blots (a Rorschach test, no doubt) and asked what they looked like. Butterflies and moths. I was shown a series of drawings and asked if there was anything wrong in them. In one a boy sawing a branch off a tree was perched on the side of the branch that was destined to fall to the ground. How dumb could you get?

Hunter drew its population from all over New York City. The alternatives were the local public school (Stuyvesant Town kids went to P.S. 40), or a private or parochial school. Hunter was a top grade education for free and it carried prestige (among those who knew about such things). Of course the school was predominantly upper-middle-class children. What other families would even know about, let alone find out how to try out for it? Most everyone was white, and most everyone was Jewish. In my class of twenty-four children, five of us were from Stuyvesant Town.

Our school facility was three floors imbedded in a building that housed Hunter College, approachable only through elevators large enough to hold our entire class at one time. We had no outside schoolyard—our building was bounded by Sixty-ninth Street on one side, Lexington Avenue and Park Avenue on the others. There was a bare rooftop terrace, fenced in like a prison camp, where we were allowed out to play. We went to the gym each day, trading our school shoes (brown oxfords or saddle shoes) for Keds sneakers. The girls wore skirts, even in gym, and tried not to bend over too far in kickball. Sometimes we went on field trips to Central Park, which was walking distance, and in those days, considered safe, though we were all warned not to speak to strangers.

When I first started Hunter Elementary School, John D'Amatio picked us up in a school bus green as frog skin. The bus started its route in Stuyvesant Town and then went uptown along First Avenue, its last stop Sutton Place, before it headed to the school to let us all off. At a fancy Sutton Place apartment building (fancy in my mind because there was an awning and a doorman) a little girl was carried out to the bus one winter morning by a father wearing a fur coat like a king's.

"Raccoon," my mother concluded after I had described it to her. He was the first man I had ever seen in a fur coat, and it seemed as much a symbol of wealth to me as anything I could imagine. No Stuyvesant Town father ever wore such a thing. I fantasized that I lived in such an apartment building—one uptown of Stuyvesant Town, where the FDR drive had the good graces to hide itself in a tunnel below street level, and the buildings backed straight up to the river itself.

At some point in the early grades, Hunter Elementary School expected its students to exhibit self-sufficiency and we were required to take public transportation to school. Mothers accompanied us till we learned the route, but later we were on our own. The little band of us who lived in Stuyvesant Town took the Twenty-third Street cross-town bus, and then changed to the Lexington Avenue bus to go uptown. After school I would wait with my friends for the Lexington Avenue southbound bus (Lexington Avenue was a two-way street in those days), stepping back from the gratings in the sidewalk when a subway train went by and our skirts blew up. I would be taking the subway to school when I entered Hunter High School, in seventh grade, but for now it was off-limits, a barely tamed animal in its subterranean cage.

My friend Elaine lived walking distance from Hunter Elementary, and when I went home with her after school, we'd cut through

Bloomingdale's at Fifty-ninth Street to get from Lexington Avenue to Third Avenue. We'd try out tester bottles of perfume, watch women being transformed by cosmetic magicians, and collect free samples of whatever we could. Impeccably coifed models, who looked like the window mannequins infused with life, promenaded the aisles, handing out tiny glass vials of Mme. Rochas or L'Air du Temps, useful for dolls after the perfume was gone. They didn't seem to notice or to mind that we were only kids. When we were older, we'd ride the escalators and venture into other departments, and when we felt particularly brave, we'd try on something, like a hat or a pair of shoes from the Sale table.

Creativity was Hunter's shtick. We wrote our autobiographies. We studied "The Epic of Man" and worked our way up from cave man, using all our senses and a lot of modeling clay. We had art and shop and music and radio workshop, where we acted out plays, and Audio Visual Enrichment, which we called by its acronym, A.V.E. Dr. Anna Curtis Chandler, an antiquated lady with tiny eyes behind monstrously thick glasses, introduced us to the great art of the world. Dr. Chandler had a gentleman admirer—a man with a flower in his buttonhole—who had been courting her, we knew, for decades. She had put her career first, this rare, squat woman, and finally married him, I learned, when she was in her eighties.

In the dark auditorium we were shown slides of the Impressionists, of Michelangelo, and Picasso. We called off their names based on clues to their style, and were able to impress everyone in a gallery when we wandered through the Metropolitan Museum. Though it was called art appreciation, I suspect what we appreciated was not so much the art as our own mastery of a warehouse of facts—something kids are good at, whether it's dinosaurs, state capitals or baseball players' batting averages.

The chief pleasure of A.V.E. by the time we were in fifth grade was the power of the darkness, the sexuality of it. The trick was to line up in such a way that when you were marched into rows you would end up sitting next to a boy whom you liked. Illuminated before us:

Renoir's luscious picnickers, Dega's ethereal ballerinas, Cezanne's oranges, and Monet's haystacks, and in the secrecy of darkness the excruciatingly close presence of a boy's forearm next to mine, hairs touching hairs.

Though we were all "gifted" children, there were some who had special gifts. Leslie had an astonishing voice and grew up, as we predicted, to be an opera singer. Elaine was able to draw animals and people as if there were a template secreted under her paper. She'd bestow her pictures upon her friends and produce special orders—swans were the great favorite. We took a proprietary interest in our classmates' special talents and rejoiced in our proximity. Though we may have envied them, when a particular talent was so obviously inaccessible to us, there was no competition. We recognized, with a kind of relief, it was all an accident of birth, just as it had been with us and our brains. There are some talents, though, that have value only in the limited societies of children. Being good at jacks or hopscotch or tossing baseball cards, unlike singing or drawing, doesn't have merit to the world at large, and it has no longevity. You can be a child who is famous among schoolmates for holding your breath, or keeping a hula hoop in motion around your waist, or balancing a paper plate on your nose, but where will that get you in the long run? Nowhere, unless there is some correlation between early, irrelevant success and success in adult life—a taste of success that inspires you forever and helps you develop the instincts and confidence of a winner.

For a long time in our class (it seemed like a year, but was probably only a few weeks) producing tinfoil curls was a talent held in highest esteem. We had no lunchroom at Hunter, so we brought sandwiches from home and ate them at our desks. We saved all the tinfoil wrappings, and smoothed the scraps flat. We rolled them around a pencil and slid them off the end, making a perfect curl. We collected these in our desks, for no purpose that I can recall. Smoothness of tinfoil was essential, but the true competition was speed.

The tinfoil mania peaked with the Linda episode. Linda was the only child in the class, in fact the only child I knew, whose parents were divorced. She bragged that as a result she got twice as many presents at her birthday (her step-parents doubling the usual output), a benefit that came as a surprise to most of us who'd heard only of the dark side of divorce, which was a rarity in our time. Linda claimed she was faster than anyone else at making tinfoil curls. Then she took it an insane step farther and claimed she was faster than all the rest of us together. She was challenged, accepted the challenge, and for that one free period after lunch, the race was on. It seemed like an obviously lopsided competition to me, but Linda was so insistent, so sure of herself that I know I wasn't the only one on the huge opposing team who thought it just possible she had a chance. She worked furiously, and we worked furiously also. It was quickly clear that Linda didn't stand a chance against us, but she wouldn't give up. The winning team worked in a state of glee, in part because success was so certain, in part because there is nothing like defeating arrogance. Though I did not slack my own pace of tinfoil rolling, I kept glancing over at Linda, doomed, outnumbered, and felt sorry for her for trapping herself in a contest which she could not possibly win. Our desks overflowed with tinfoil curls, compared to her modest pile, but still she would not admit defeat. When our free time was over, though the evidence was incontrovertible, she insisted on counting them out. Exhausted, in tears, she was taken from the room by a teacher and in the future we were forbidden this most innocent of pastimes.

What made some children attractive and others outcasts? Details too subtle for any adult to comprehend. As I look at our old class pictures with the objective eye of an adult, the boys in our class all the girls thought cute were no better looking than the losers, and the girls who were considered pretty were not marked by beauty or size of hairbow. It had as much to do with self-confidence, your own estimate of your status, as anything else. It also had to do with smells and secretions and body type. Fat children were doomed, as were children who had perpetually runny noses or flaking skin, those who left things hanging out of their noses, picked their noses, ate what they picked, chewed the skin on the sides of their nails so they bled, had wax in their ears, or passed air.

I was popular in school—often voted class president—but my political success depended on a faithful band of male followers, mostly outcasts, whom I was constantly trying to avoid. One boy six inches shorter than me, would kiss my chair every morning as he took it off the desk, and at the end of the day when he turned it, legs in the air, up on the desk so the floor could be mopped. His idolization annoyed me so much I once punched him in the nose and gave him a nosebleed, the only time I ever punched anyone in my whole life. In an afterschool conference (no doubt insisted upon by his mother), the teacher, my mother, his mother, I and he faced off. Forced to, I said I was sorry, but when asked to explain my action I said, plainly, "I can't stand him," though he gazed at me with the same huge, adoring eyes. He hadn't learned the virtues of playing hard to get, nor had anyone discovered the concept of sexual harassment.

Fifteen years later he invited me to his Princeton Senior Prom. We hadn't seen each other for years. I went out of curiosity and with a certain amount of nostalgia for my childhood. He was twice as tall as he had been and smoked a pipe, but though he had grown up into a decent adult I found I was no more eager for his attentions than I had been when I was six.

The boy I liked best seemed to like me, too, although in a memoir he wrote (under a pseudonym) as an adult, he detailed his development as a homosexual. I wonder now what he was really feeling when his fingers found mine in the dark of A.V.E., and we clutched hands and held our breath, while we stared at the masterpieces on the screen, or when he dusted the chalk off the blackboard with the top of his crewcut to impress me. (It did.)

Once a week, for a season, our entire grade went to afterschool social dancing classes at Viola Wolf studios, a short walk from Hunter. Parents paid for these lessons, and scholarships must have been available, for everyone went. In the mirrored ballroom, lined with gilt chairs with red velvet seats, on a wooden floor as vast as a lake, we worked our way through the waltz, the fox trot, the tango, the cha-cha, and culminated in the lindy, the dance of our time. We girls wore party dresses, patent leather shoes, and white anklet socks, except for Linda, who wore stockings. In a kindness to my friend Barbara, who wore white gloves to hide the warts on her hands, I wore gloves also (a kindness that was no doubt inspired, if not imposed upon me, by my mother). At Viola Wolf all the rivalries were intensified, all the passions kindled in A.V.E. were brought out into the light. Boys dashed across the dance floor to claim their partners, as girls did for the ladies' choice. My coterie of male followers, the shortest at the head of the pack, too often reached me before one of the boys whom I preferred.

At the end of sixth grade our social lives came to an abrupt halt. All the girls at Hunter Elementary School, with few exceptions, went on to Hunter College High School. The boys went to private schools like Horace Mann, or attended public junior high for two years, before entering Stuyvesant High School, Hunter's all-male equivalent, where my mother eventually taught.

The lost bet, 1955

X

PHONES

During the day, in anything close to decent weather, Stuyvesant Town mommies gathered on the benches by the playgrounds where their children played. They frequented the same spot, year after year, until their children were grown. Day care and the idea of formal "play groups" didn't exist then, but the benchsitters kept an eye on each other's kids while any one of them was absent. They were an interchangeable headquarters of mommies, providing provisions (juice and crackers), authority ("no standing on the swings!"), and arbitration if a game of potsy ended in dispute. While the children played, the mommies talked and knitted. They were, for the most part, college-educated women, yet my mother was one of the few who saw child-rearing as a hiatus in her career.

Once I was in school all day my mother resigned her position on the bench. Her friendships flourished on the telephone. Friendship seemed, as I was growing up, very much the enterprise of women. Men might have a buddy from their college days or The War, but contact was usually limited to Christmas cards (most often sent out by wives) or an occasional visit if they happened to be in town. All my parents' friends were couples, outgrowths of my mother's friendships with other women. This seemed true of most of the families I knew. The husbands endured each other, or actually liked each other, but their relationships depended entirely on their wives' connection. The Greek furriers my father ate lunch with every day had little to do with his life beyond that noon hour. In my entire childhood I don't remember my father ever once having a conversation on the telephone with a friend. The rare phone calls he got were usually patients in distress.

Not so, my mother. Every night, after the dinner dishes were washed and put away, she would retire to her bedroom and get on the phone. Sometimes she called her friends, sometimes they called her. Some she was in touch with at least once a month, some once a week, and some every day. To discourage herself from talking too long, she sat in a wooden armchair, without a cushion. The phone was right beside the bed, but her bed had a lace bedspread on it, and was for looking at, not lounging on (a constant source of contention between us).

I used my mother's telephone time as an opportunity to rummage through her dresser drawers. The top one had jewelry, dress gloves that were never worn, and scarves that had been folded so long the creases seemed to have become part of the fabric. To confuse thieves, my mother mixed good jewelry in with the junk jewelry, and part of my amusement was to separate the pieces out by hunting for the little stamp that said 14K or 18K, Sterling or 800.

The bottom dresser drawer had unused gifts to be passed on to someone else (like hankies with embroidered violets) and gifts that she would not part with but she considered too good to use: a beaded purse, expensive perfume, an organdy apron, and cream-colored, oval soaps in a box lined with doilies. Also in this drawer were mementos from weddings, christenings, and bar mitzvahs and all the gifts I had made for her—some school projects, some inspired by *McCall's Giant Make-it-Book,* a volume that bristled with promise for me. Included in the collection was a pincushion shaped like a pear, a felt eyeglass case decorated with sequins, a washcloth folded to look like a cat perched on a bar of soap, several "lipstick ladies," which were papier-mâché dolls' heads applied to Woolworth lipstick, a collection of poems I had written all neatly copied out in a cloth-bound book, and a coupon book of favors, never redeemed, for things like "breakfast in bed" and "half hour peace on the phone."

All these things were there, preserved, untouched, when I went to clean out my mother's things after her death, including wedding souvenirs from four failed marriages—an engraved matchbook from one cousin, a glass toothpick holder from another, a place card from a third, and sugar-covered almonds, hard as marbles, tied up in white netting, from my own first marriage. In the closet I discovered more sugar-covered almonds, a whole cache of them in white boxes with wax flowers on top, souvenirs of my parents' wedding. Had they ordered a dozen extra to save for posterity, or were these all relics of guests who had never shown up?

While my mother talked on the phone she looked up occasionally and told me to stop pulling things apart, but I continued modeling jewelry, trying on gloves. When my mother had settled into deep conversation I'd dig through the drawer in her desk where she kept cosmetics and experiment with the eyeshadow she rarely used and the lipstick which she applied anytime she left the house.

My mother chatted with her friends and laughed with them in a way that was different from her interactions with her family. I eavesdropped attentively. I learned about my mother, this other side of her, and I learned about her views on our lives, and my own doings. I heard about which trivial aspects of the day took on status in her anecdotes, which were never spoken of. She bragged about me far more than she ever complimented me, and though she was always telling me about the intensity of her love for me, it was when she talked to her friends about me that I heard about her pride.

The phone was installed in my parents' bedroom, at the far end of the apartment, its ringer was on the wall in the dining area. When the phone rang during dinner, I would run down the long hall to get it, with my father shouting after me, "Tell them we'll call back when we're done eating," and my mother following me to the bedroom, saying to my father, before she followed me down the hall, "I'll just say hello for now."

When my mother had taken over the receiver and I returned to the table my father would ask, "So who was it?" and then groan when I told him.

"Well that's good for half an hour at least," he'd say of one friend, or "that's good for an hour," if it was her best friend, Ruth. When he'd finish his coffee he'd repair to the living room and read the comics in *The New York World Telegram and Sun,* while I perched on the chair and read over his shoulder. He never cleared the table or attempted to wash a dish, but it was not punishment to my mother for deserting us for her friends, but rather the fact that it never occurred to him to do so.

My mother kept in regular touch with her friends from Barnard College, friends from work, her elderly godmother, and friends who were mothers of school friends of mine from Hunter. These Hunter mothers were a ferocious bunch. Together they were a united force, working for the good of all their daughters in the school, yet among themselves they were constantly pitting us against each other. They called to compare how their daughters had done on tests, to compare their progress on homework, to compare their success at art, shop, and even gym. It is utterly remarkable that our friendships survived our mothers' competitiveness.

Once Carol Jean's mother, Cornelia, called my mother up so my mother could hear Carol Jean practicing the piano in the background. I was summoned to listen. Carol Jean was always a piece ahead of me in the piano book.

"Like silver bells" my mother said, repeating Cornelia's words, with a look that reminded me that, unlike me, Carol was no sluggard about practicing, and the results of her devotion had paid off.

"Well I play like golden bells," I screamed as I ran off, wondering at the same time whether golden bells or silver bells had a superior sound.

When Elsie got Elaine lunchbags—white with her name printed on them in black Bodoni Bold—my mother got them for me, as well. When I got velvet party shoes at Lord & Taylor, Elsie got them for Elaine.

Once Elsie called my mother up to inform her of a recent discovery. When I had been over to play that afternoon I had drawn an angel with ballpoint pen on a piece of paper. The pen point had gone through and scratched the finish on a dresser top. (Elaine had remembered to put a magazine under her own paper.) My mother apologized endlessly to Elsie and yelled at me—a common pattern. Elaine's parents had given her their bedroom in their one-bedroom apartment (they slept in the living room) and we had to play there, among land mines of mahogany. Sometimes I took the fall for Elaine, who tiptoed around her demanding mother and when necessary, resorted to the art of lying for self-protection.

If I was a scamp compared to Elaine, my friend Barbara was a scamp compared to me. Elaine was small and cautious; Barbara was big and fearless. Jane, Barbara's mother, seemed free of the competitive instincts of the other mothers, and faced her daughter's transgressions with good-humored resignation. In later years she laughed when she summed up our different styles: "Elaine kept her dolls on the shelf, Cory kept her dolls on the bed, Barbara kept her dolls under the bed." Indeed, Elaine's dolls had their original hairdos intact, while most of Barbara's had braids undone, curls clipped, and in one case where a desk lamp had been employed as a hair dryer, the hair had been completely burnt off.

I told my mother everything in those days. She told me everything, too. She was, I believe, hungry for a sister. And missed her own mother, to whom, she told me—long after I grew up and did not confide in her completely any more—she told everything. I carried some of these secrets she confided in me as burdens. I knew, for instance, three girls who were adopted—and only one of them knew herself. I knew that my teacher had written to another teacher that I was her favorite pupil. I knew that a friend who was black had tried to scrub her skin to get all the dark color off. I knew that a friend masturbated in bed and her mother was worried about her. I never told these secrets.

My mother spent more time on the telephone every night talking to friends than she spent talking with my father. These voices were

the constant companions of her life, though she did not see the actual people that often. My mother had a few good friends who lived
far away, but she rarely spoke to them on the phone. Those friendships were sustained in letters—my mother's script as familiar to me
as her voice. When my mother died, friends from different parts of
her life came to her memorial service, the real people, together in the
same room for the first time ever.

Long-distance calls in those days had a quality of miracle to
them—like that first wire Marconi sent across the Atlantic to a waiting British monarch. At least once a year, especially around Thanksgiving and Christmas, my parents would make ritual calls to Uncle
Appy in California and Uncle John in Indiana. After the grownups
were done catching up, the phone would be passed on to the children. As much as I was thrilled to have any contact with my distant
cousins, these calls were agonies. I never knew what to say, and neither did they, so we would hold the phone for minutes that cost as
much as gold, repeating the word "hello" and giggling. While
grownups are perfectly able to resume acquaintances after a long hiatus, children are naturally shy of each other. With relatives they
haven't seen for a long time they take a while to check each other out,
to make friends all over again. When pressed to speak, we said inane
things like "What are you doing now?" Response: "Talking on the
phone" (more giggles). Grownups will ask their standard big questions "What grade are you in now?" or "What are you learning in
school?" but children stick closer to the minute, the unimportant details of the meal they just ate. A few seconds of phone line time with
either of my two older male cousins whom I knew practically not at
all, but maintained crushes on, was enough to render me speech-
less—all the worse because my parents were always hovering right by,
urging me to speak up, reminding me of the cost of every incredible
transcontinental breath.

If talking on the telephone was, in my father's view, my
mother's chief vice, one my father was totally innocent of, it would
be only fair to point out what she thought were his.

My father's office was down the block from a hardware store owned and managed by a man named Getz. My father dropped by there almost every day, gabbed with Getz and the men who hung out there, prowled among the stuff, and came home with a new widget, which he showed off at dinner. A drawer in the kitchen we called "the jungle drawer" was filled with these acquisitions—washers, screw anchors, short-handled screwdrivers, socket wrenches.

My father's other vice was cigars. He smoked them in the house. Worse, he smoked them in the car, in spite of my mother's nagging, and my exaggerated gagging noises. I can't believe he really liked cigars; I think they were one thing he clung to, to spite my mother. When she accused him of moral weakness—"a child with a pacifier," she said—he vowed to prove her wrong.

"If I give up smoking from this day for a year what will you do?" he challenged her.

"I will kiss the floor," she said.

And she did, one year later. I photographed her on her knees, her lips actually on the grey wall-to-wall carpeting in the dining area, right where I had spilled countless glasses of milk, walked with muddy boots, and once, worst of all, spilled a whole jar of red poster paint, which never washed out and ruined the carpeting, in fact our whole apartment, forever.

XI

SHOPPING

Shopping was the province of women. That was the way it was in my family, and in all other families I knew. Women shopped for the food, the clothes, the furniture. If men bought anything, it was the family car. My mother complained that she had to do all the shopping, but my father's shopping acumen was so low she rarely entrusted him with a mission more important than the Sunday morning run to the bakery (with a handwritten list) and the newsstand for the Sunday *Times*. The only lapse I remember was once, when I was around seven, she sent him off to buy me a pair of shoes for school. Her expectation was a pair of brown oxfords or saddle shoes. My father, who had never mastered the distinction between dress and school shoes, in his innocence indulged me in a pair of green alligator Mary Janes. My mother instructed him to take them right back, but in a rare show of defiance, he insisted I be allowed to keep them. They were a delight of my childhood, as atypical, as outrageous, as if they belonged to the witch in the Wizard of Oz.

For his own wardrobe, my father was taken shopping by my mother. She had decided that as a dentist he had to look respectable at all times, and often sent him back to adjust his attire if she felt he wasn't dressed properly—which, left on his own, he never was. Only on weekends in the country, where he "wouldn't be seen" could he wear what he wanted, and in his bedroom in the house that had been my grandfather's in Mt. Kisco, he kept an entire closet of comfortable, worn, out-of-style garments that he wasn't allowed to wear anywhere else.

No wonder my father hated shopping for clothes for himself. The men's departments were endless racks of drab colors. The Hong Kong tailor, where he got suits and monogrammed shirts, a windowless room with buzzing fluorescent lights. My father, shackled, with cuffs billowing around his ankles, chalk marks on his sleeves, caught my eye in the mirror and winked.

"Look what I have to put up with for your mother," he said.

But in fact it was more than my mother that forced my father into this, it was what being an adult required. It was the burden of being a man.

There was only one occasion when my father had to go shopping without my mother's aid, and that was when he needed to buy her a present. He was a dismal failure. Early in their marriage he had been traumatized by The Bra. While stationed in Paris during The War, he'd foolishly ventured into a fancy lingerie shop to send my mother a gift. He selected a black lace bra, and when asked the size, he pointed to the salesgirl and said, "like you."

The bra was not only something my mother would never choose—she wore sturdy white elastic and cotton—but was ridiculously small. My mother was as offended and amused by the bra's inappropriateness as by my father's apparent ignorance about her size, especially since he professed to admire her well-endowed body.

"A little, flat-chested French girl!" she said, as she dangled the wisp of a thing, holding it straight-armed, away from her body.

I suspect it was not only that my father's French language skills failed him, but that his embarrassment overwhelmed him. He never really dared look at the bra or the salesgirl's bosom. But the truth was, no matter what he bought my mother, he was certain it would be something she wouldn't like or that wouldn't fit. If he gave her a sweater or a blouse with the price-tag removed so she couldn't return it, he would be in trouble, but if he left the price tag on she would chide him for how much he had spent. Once I had helped my father select a nightgown for my mother. She kept it, but said it was too good to wear. It was there, in her bottom dresser drawer, still folded on its original creases, after she died.

If our apartment was small, there were many large public spaces that were part of my indoor landscape, department stores in particular. They were permanent institutions, solid as churches. I knew their layouts perfectly, the locations of the ladies' rooms and water fountains, the best routes to maneuver around crowds at the height of the Christmas rush.

The three department stores we patronized on Thirty-fourth Street each had a distinct character. Altman's, on Fifth Avenue, was patrician, with high ceilings, red carpet runners, polished wood floors, a hush over everything. Customers were sparse and moved at a genteel pace. The first floor smelled of leather and perfume. Price tags of many items in display cases, were, incomprehensibly, only legible if you contorted yourself and read upside down through the glass shelf, or were entirely obscured under the article for sale. Upstairs the dressing rooms were the size of our Stuyvesant Town kitchen, with three-way mirrors that let me see the sides of me that were usually as hidden from my own view as the far side of the moon.

Orbach's, half a block west on Thirty-fourth Street, was packed with customers, who scurried, pushed, and grabbed. Garments were spread promiscuously on open tables. You had to paw through mounds of panties or tangles of bras to find what you wanted. At Altman's you refined your sense of quality, then you went to Orbach's to hunt for the same things for less.

On an entire city block of its own was Macy's, The World's Largest Store. It was thorough and honest and straightforward. Nearby Gimbels and Saks 34th appealed to the same market, but my mother would no sooner have bought anything in Gimbels than she would have voted for a Republican. Store loyalty was as immutable as brand loyalty. (The people we knew who bought Fords would never buy Chevies; Chevy people would never buy Fords.) In Macy's furniture department there were model rooms—three-sided rooms, like my dollhouse, with the front wall missing. There were real glass windows that looked out on tromp l'oeil pastures, woodlands, or cityscapes, or sometimes a twilight so real I wondered if the outside wall of Macy's had been opened up to the sky. Each room had a theme and a color scheme, like a stage set. There was a Renaissance bedroom with a canopy bed with red velvet draperies, a living room that resembled a white-washed Italian villa, a library that looked as if it belonged in an English manor house. Our Stuyvesant Town apartment, in contrast, was just a sad accumulation of furniture. I wanted to sit on those plush sofas, lie down on those elegant beds, peek inside the drawers of those dressers. One time I actually slipped under the velvet rope and stood on the forbidden side, but I did not dare do more than that.

Once I had heard a no-doubt apocryphal story about a child who had crawled into and fallen asleep in the teepee in the Museum of Natural History. He had awakened there after hours to be able to roam the museum and look at—and touch—anything he wanted. This was my fantasy about stores, that I would have them all to myself, after hours. Never mind that it was unlikely my mother would lose me or leave me behind in any store, nor that the store would likely be dark and scary, and patrolled by guard dogs with fangs. My favorite fantasy was of F.A.O. Schwartz. I imagined unfettering the dolls from their stands, reaching into the secret recesses of the enormous dollhouse, and climbing on the backs of the Steiff animals that were large as life.

For regular shopping trips, my mother and I took the bus uptown, but when my mother was doing a big shopping, my father would "give up a Saturday" and play chauffeur. While he sat in the car in the no-parking, loading zone area of Thirty-fifth Street, he read the paper, did the crossword puzzle, studied books on chess, smoked his pipe, and struck up conversations with the cop on the beat or the store security man. On occasion they felt sorry for him, a beleaguered male, and kept their eye on the car for him while he ran to get himself a cup of coffee.

On one occasion, it was my mother who rescued him. He had left the car, trusting his luck, and came back just as a cop was starting to write up a ticket. My mother and I emerged from the back door of Macy's, our arms full of packages. The cop looked up at us.

"Mrs. Demas!" he cried out. He had been a student of hers at Stuyvesant High School. He hugged my mother, tore up the ticket, and helped load our shopping in the car.

"Don't worry, " said my father, laughing, "it will all go back in the morning," for my mother was famous for returning and exchanging things.

At least once each season we made an excursion to the department stores of upper Fifth Avenue: Saks Fifth Avenue, Lord & Taylor, and Best & Co. My mother wouldn't buy anything for herself at these "costly" places, but she would buy my "good" winter coat there, my party dress, and fancy shoes. I always felt as if we didn't quite belong in these stores, my mother in her serviceable cloth coat among the other women in their full-length minks, but my mother was never intimidated.

"They want our money, just like any other business," she said. The saleswomen always seemed like temporarily impoverished countesses, who treated us with polite disdain. Their "May I help you?" sounded accusatory. But my mother had no sympathy with my discomfort.

"If they were better educated, they wouldn't end up as saleswomen in a department store."

At Fifth Avenue department stores your purchases were folded with intricate care and settled in billows of tissue paper in crisp boxes. The endless quantities of tissue paper of those stores—white and fresh, never a wrinkle, never a smudge. You could plunge into all that whiteness as if it were a drift of new-fallen snow. You carried home the boxes inside shopping bags with the store's name imprinted in fancy gold lettering. You always tried to get a maximum of bags—one for every box—for you used them again and again. You'd take them with you on future shopping trips to less prestigious stores, and tuck the dingy bags down into their depths. Stuyvesant Town women were competitive about their bargain-hunting skills; nevertheless, they flaunted their status symbol shopping bags.

My father—like most men, my mother thought—was oblivious to the class distinctions of stores. Once he was even caught throwing garbage into a Saks Fifth Avenue shopping bag from my mother's collection.

Right along Fifth Avenue, in the shadow of Rockefeller Center and St. Patrick's Cathedral, sidewalk vendors sold hot dogs or roasted chestnuts. They were territorial, and when pushed on by the cops (harassment seemed part of the beat policeman's duty) they wearily moved their carts, but when the coast was clear, they circulated back to their original spots.

The hot dog vendors were often Greeks, brought over by some Americanized cousin from his village. They had orange umbrellas above their carts, like umbrellas on a beach they might never see again. Even though it was our family friend's business that supplied the hot dogs and rolls, it was rare that my mother let me have one. She was suspicious about processed meat. These hot dogs, sometimes rubbery, sometimes leathery, always tasted more delicious for being forbidden. The sauerkraut spilled over them like seaweed. The mustard was alarmingly bright, and no matter how careful I was, inevitably got on my cuff.

The smell of the roasting chestnuts, though, even my mother couldn't resist. The chestnut men stood by their little charcoal fires, rural peasants transported to a modern metropolis. They were refugees from another time period, characters from a Dickens novel. Though just steps away, they were a world away from the perfumed calm of the Saks Fifth Avenue lobby, or the rapturous glory of the inside of St. Patrick's. Stoic, and to my mind, tragic, they were there even in the worst of winter, swaddled in old clothing, with the blackened faces of coal miners or chimney sweeps. A little bag of chestnuts cost a quarter. The shells were black as charcoal, and I was always so impatient to eat them I invariably burnt my fingers and my tongue. The chestnut was moist and hot as a living creature.

It was an incidental consequence of World War II that I was able to feel at home at the ritziest store on Fifth Avenue: Tiffany's. While my father was stationed in Germany, a sergeant in his outfit (in my father's stories it was always the sergeants who precipitated adventures) announced that high prices were being paid for American watches, and persuaded my father to entrust him with his eleven dollar watch. The sergeant wasn't heard from again for the duration of the war, which my father survived without a timepiece. My mother chastised him for his gullibility, but my father was vindicated in the end. Back home, the war over, a baby (me) on the way, he received a letter. All it said was, "Quit your bitching, here's your money," enclosed with a check for $125. My father went off to Tiffany's, a store he'd never ventured inside of before. For $125 he got a solid gold Tiffany watch, and had it engraved on the back "June 1947," my mother's due date. Unfortunately, I was born a month early, in May. My father, who hoped to consult his watch so that he would never forget the birthday of his first (and only) offspring, never could get it right. But the watch gave me a sense as a child that our family had a vested interest in Tiffany's, and when we brought the watch in for its periodic repair work, I browsed the aisles and felt that I belonged. My father has since passed the watch on to me and is content again with a cheap watch that tells the time and date more reliably than the Tiffany's watch, and also never requires the arduousness of winding.

At the other end of the shopping spectrum from Tiffany's, and at the other end of Manhattan, down on Fourteenth Street, was S. Klein on the Square. I never learned what the "S" stood for, but the square in question was Union Square. It was not a park my mother would linger in, and if she had to traverse it she did so with quick steps and her pocketbook snug against her side. The benches were occupied by vagrants, and unsavory characters of all varieties wandered about, ready to prey (or so I fancied) on the innocent bourgeoisie. There were often orators standing on crates (a generation before, they would have been soapboxes) passionately haranguing a ragtag group of onlookers about some issue, political or religious.

"Nuts," my mother said firmly and marched me briskly past.

S. Klein was a collection of buildings, all painted grey to look like one edifice. You could tell when you passed from one building to another because the floor changed levels. I learned from my mother how to navigate through the tunnels of merchandise. Clothing that was not hung up on great long metal pipes was dumped out on wooden tables with edges like animal troughs. Even Orbach's was palatial compared to Klein's. Everything about Klein's had an aura of poverty: the dim lighting, the low ceilings, the dull linoleum on the floors. In the communal try-on room women in dingy girdles and brassieres struggled into garments and squinted at themselves in the narrow, cloudy mirrors. Everyone pretended not to be looking at each other. No sleek boxes, no tissue paper, no shopping bags with handles, just thin paper bags in dismal grey. Yet my mother endured S. Klein's—as did legions of other Stuyvesant Town matrons— because an astute shopper could discover a dress that Saks would carry, at a fraction of the price.

Was shopping really a necessity of life, or was it something created, a pastime, like playing cards? In any case, countless hours of my childhood were consumed by the perpetual industry of acquisition.

My mother, untrue to the female stereotype, took no pleasure in shopping. She faced it with the same resignation she faced all domestic chores, and she applied to it her usual standards of perfection. She was not content to buy the exact item she wanted, she was satisfied only if she got it for the best price possible. The principle often overrode her wisdom. If she bought something and then saw it for less elsewhere, she would return it to the first store and buy it at the second, even if the price of carfare negated the savings. As for her time, she valued that at nothing. She was a conscript in the great Merchandise War, the little Shoppers, "us," against the great Stores, "them." It required constant vigilance and energy.

My mother had one good friend in Stuyvesant Town, Barbara's mother, Jane, who chronically paid list price for things, a condition incurred, my mother contended, by her not being Jewish (or Greek). Not only did Jane lack a primal urge to strike a bargain, but she didn't suffer guilt for not doing so. She had even admitted to my mother that on occasion, when she went shopping, she took a cab. The idea of a taxi was such anathema to my mother that she was reluctant to take one even when it was demonstrated to be cheaper than busfare (given the number of passengers and the shortness of the trip).

My mother had a peculiar discomfort with spending money. She constantly talked about refurnishing the apartment, but she could never actually bring herself to do it.

"It's because I grew up in the Depression," she said, but I think there was something more to it. A sense, perhaps, of the basic frivolity of material things, and a deeply entrenched dislike of anything that seemed self-indulgent. Although she regularly indulged me, she never, in my whole life with her, bought anything for herself because she simply wanted it.

XII

GIRLS

Hunter College High School still exists today, but it's a different creature from the junior-senior high school I entered in 1958, when I was eleven. My teachers are all retired or dead, there's a new building, uptown, and, most striking, half of the students now are boys.

It makes me wonder what a school really is. The concept of the school—its curriculum, priorities, and rules—and its reputation will change over time. If the student body is evanescent, the faculty mortal, then all you have that is tangible is the physical plant.

Hunter High School was housed in a pseudo-medieval castle, a style favored by New York public schools, attached, like an architectural relic, to the modern edifice of Hunter College. The high school building faced the bustle of Lexington Avenue, between Sixty-eighth and Sixty-ninth Streets, the college faced more subdued Park Avenue.

There were high ceilings, light fixtures dangling from chains, and tall gothic-style windows that could be opened at the top by the dexterous use of window poles. Like many city buildings that had endured decades of pollution, its limestone surface was blackened, as if it had gone through a war. There was decorative stonework at the top, barely visible from the street below: crenellations, ersatz balconies, and gargoyles the size of kindergartners. When some of this started crumbling, the stonework was removed. For months—could it have been years?—the school was encased in scaffolding, while workmen slowly amputated gargoyles and acanthus leaves. We looked out at the world through metal bars. In early fall, on one of the balconies of the apartment house across Lexington Avenue, a gentleman in a dressing gown was served coffee by a maid in uniform. Sitting among evergreens and topiary too perfect to be real, he read his morning paper, oblivious to the traffic below and the eyes of the students imprisoned across the street.

At the time there was no other public school in America quite like Hunter. Take fifteen hundred adolescent girls, selected through entrance examinations, drag them from all five boroughs of New York City (a large contingent from Stuyvesant Town), provide them with challenging courses, and let them compete.

And compete we did, from grade seven through twelve. There were no remedial classes, no gut courses. We were graded on a scale of 0 to 100. Though no one ever got a hundred in any subject, anything below an 85 was considered failure. Grade point averages were calculated to the hundredth of a decimal point, and class rank was recalculated every marking period, which seemed to occur remarkably often. One classmate stopped by the office regularly to check on hers. Was it possible that somehow while we slept some student had improved a grade in some course and so altered her class standing and therefore yours? You weren't told anyone's else's standing, of course, just your own. The less confident confined our inquiries to times we were sure no one would overhear.

Hunter raised us to believe there was a clear path that led from good grades, to acceptance to the best college, to the best life. How much easier to believe happiness depends on a simple goal—like a high grade point average—than to have it be something less well defined. We all undoubtedly discovered later how narrow Hunter's vision was, but even the most rebellious of us bought into the priorities at the time. This drive for academic success channeled our hormonal activity, to the extent that we were practically unaware of it. If our bodies were crying out, we threw ourselves into our work and into the passionate social structure of Hunter High School, the extracur-

ricular activities—the school publications, the literary magazine, social service organizations, and the General Organization ("G.O."), a
student senate where issues of small consequence were fiercely debated
on a weekly basis. There was no prom committee at Hunter, but there
was a French literary magazine. There were no athletic teams, but
there was the International Relations Club.

Without boys for us to compete for, we strove for popularity
among girls. Leadership positions in the myriad of student organizations were hotly contested. A girl's popularity became most obvious
at her birthday, when tradition dictated the giving of corsages. A florist
shop had strategically located itself across the street from Hunter and
was always a flurry of activity in the morning before school. A popular girl might be endowed with a dozen corsages—sometimes not just
the fifty-cent carnations but roses, or even an orchid, if a bunch of
friends chipped in. When she had covered all available front of blouse
surface with corsages, she sported some on her back. Some girls rigged
up sandwich board contraptions out of poster board to accommodate
the abundance. During class change time you were always passing people on the stairs bedecked in flowers, not one of them given by a boy.

We wore our corsages home on the subway and bus, no doubt
to the bewilderment of other travelers. Even though I laid mine tenderly in the refrigerator shelf, they wilted in a day or two. Propelled
by this vast waste, as well as an impending deadline, when I was Editor of *What's What* (the school newspaper) I wrote an editorial that
proposed substituting the giving of corsages with the giving of pa-
perback books. I argued books were not only more lasting but less
ostentatious. Of course no one heeded my appeal. Corsages were valued precisely because of their evanescence, and because they were
badges of popularity.

Hunter girls came from all over New York City. Some walked,
some had hour-long commutes on a variety of buses and subways,
and occasionally even the Staten Island Ferry. The households they
came from were as economically varied as New York itself. Some girls'

fathers were wealthy lawyers, some didn't have fathers at all. Some lived in luxurious apartments overlooking Central Park and vacationed in Switzerland, others lived in tiny walkups and never went on vacations anywhere. Fortunately—miraculously?—these differences didn't have much bearing on the social life of the school. What we cared about most was how we performed at Hunter—who did the best science project, who got the lead in the dramatic society play, who got 800s on her SATs.

Hunter girls who lived in Stuyvesant Town often made arrangements to travel back and forth to school together. Even if you didn't, the chances were fairly good that you'd run into schoolmates on the Twenty-third Street cross-town bus, or waiting on the platform for the Lexington Avenue subway. I was chronically late. I hated to get up in the morning—no doubt because I was often up long after bedtime reading novels (The Brontes and Thomas Hardy were popular among us), and because I was anxious about school, for I was often behind in my homework and studying, no doubt from reading novels at my desk instead of doing my schoolwork. For a period of time a friend, whom my father called the Eager Beaver, used to stop by our apartment to pick me up. Sometimes she would arrive early enough to exhort me to dress faster, gobble down my cereal. She sought my company less, I think, for the pleasure of my companionship than for the opportunity to have someone to check over her answers on the calculus homework and quiz her for the upcoming French test. Sometimes I used my travel time to finish my homework. If I didn't get a seat on the subway, I could wedge my three-ring binder in between the bodies crowded into the car, and have a desk standing up.

I know I'm not the only Hunter alumna who still occasionally has nightmares about arriving late to school. We were required to leave our coats in our lockers before classes began, but since that was in the basement, an extra flight down and up, I would often race straight to class. The worst mornings were those when my first period class was on the fifth floor and I had to run up all the stairs, hoping to slide into my seat before the bell rang, hoping the teacher wouldn't see my coat and send me to down my locker, as well as to the office for a late pass.

While the typical suburban American public high school of the sixties was low and sprawling, Hunter was resolute in its verticality. There were six floors, with the gym at the top, the elevator reserved for teachers and for students with coveted medical passes. We had five minutes between classes. Traffic on the stairs was intense, and knitting needles were banned. (It was never clear if that was really to prevent someone from being impaled during class change time or if it was to prevent the distraction of knitting—a popular activity at the time—during class.) Urban backpacks hadn't been invented yet, and we dragged our books around in giant tote bags. There was a hardcover text for each class, all school property, clothed in book covers made from brown bags from D'Agostino's turned inside out, the pages softened by the sweat of several decades of previous scholars. No one would have believed that a generation later women would climb stairs in place as a voluntary form of exercise. This was a time when few women did any exercise at all by choice, and for most Hunter girls gym was the low point of the week. We were a physically unfit group of young ladies, but not the least concerned about it. I remember a girl weeping because she had broken a fingernail on a basketball.

There were two gymnasiums on the sixth floor, mirror images, with changing rooms and a foyer in between. When the federal government's Physical Fitness Tests were held, for the distance race, we had to run from the end of one gym to the end of the other, a perfect New York City block. For some evaluation, whose purpose remains an enigma, all three hundred members of my class had to line up by size place, a line that led from gym to gym. I turned out to be 150th, which meant, I guess, that 5'4 ½" inches was our median height. There were no outside playing fields at Hunter, not a single inch of green turf or even paved yard. The only time we had an outdoor activity was our yearly field trip to Central Park's Sheep Meadow, where some competed in interclass races while others held their faces up towards the Fifth Avenue skyline, hoping to acquire a tan.

For gym we wore one-piece navy blue outfits with bloomer bottoms, a style unchanged from our mothers' day. Our names had to be embroidered in white over our left breast, like a garage mechanic's. The gym suits were comically ugly, but we found them merely mortifying. The worst nightmare was to be caught at gym during a fire drill and to have to line up outside on Lexington Avenue, where total strangers—possibly even boys!—would see us.

There weren't many in my class who had much experience with members of the opposite sex. A few girls stood around at the corner after school, by the entrance to the Lexington Avenue IRT, and were seen in the company of boys—boys who went to some Catholic high school, or maybe even no school at all. On occasion they were observed smoking cigarettes. A few girls were cheerleaders for Stuyvesant High School. At the occasional football game I attended with a group of Hunter friends, I watched them perform. In their little skirts, legs naked, breasts bouncing behind the white sweaters, they seemed to belong to a different world, too remote for me to feel envy. Or if I did, I didn't admit it to myself.

On warm spring evenings, while I toiled over homework in my room, I would hear laughter outside, eleven stories below, and go to the window to look. In the building diagonally across from me, the Stuyvesant High School boy I had a crush on was in his room toiling over his homework. Down by the street light a group of teenagers who went to the local high school—rather than Hunter or Stuyvesant—would be hanging out. It is amazing how clearly I could see and hear them, how quiet lay the rest of the city. They were talking, teasing, laughing, and more—they were kissing! Yes, there was a girl I knew making out with her boyfriend. They were under a streetlight. To show off, my mother said, when she once looked out and saw them, or was it because it was safe there, just as it was safe in the proximity of a group?

I wanted to ignore them, but I would keep getting up from my desk. I pressed close to the side of the window, for I would have never let them know I watched them. I felt superior—after all, what kind of girl makes out like that with boys?—yet I was insatiably curious.

My own adolescent experiences with boys were few, and perhaps because of that, their intensity was heightened, their vividness in memory more acute. At a party I met a friend's cousin named Alex, who discovered in our conversation that I had not seen the movie *West Side Story.* He promised to remedy this, and he did so, by inviting me out on a date. The film was playing at Radio City Music Hall, a setting that was perfect in its grandeur for my heightened emotion, as was the passion of the story on the screen. Our kiss goodnight, inside the front door of the apartment, was the culminating perfection of the evening, until my father—perhaps urged to by my mother who was concerned about our activities in the darkened foyer—chose that moment to pass through on his way to the kitchen to get an apple. We stood, frozen, in the dark while my father fumbled in the refrigerator and rinsed off his selected specimen at the sink. I could hear his teeth piercing the skin of the apple and sinking into its flesh.

Alex never did ask me out on a date again, though he called me once to talk.

"It's a long subway ride from where he lives in Queens," said my mother, to cheer me up, and I hated her for knowing that in spite of all my efforts to show I didn't care, I cared about little else, for weeks.

Hunter girls may have had little hands-on experience with sex, but we were certainly provided with a thorough sexual education. Sex hygiene was a required course, peculiarly the domain of the gym teachers. We were required to memorize quantities of information that most of us would not put to use for years. I studied lists of methods of contraception and was puzzled by my parents' hilarity at finding "Baggies" included as an emergency barrier method. It was only later that I understood what was funny about a classmate's earnest question at the end of a lecture on sodomy, "do they jail the animals?"

We were a school of virgins, our virginity keeping our brains intact, perhaps. A considerable amount of sexual energy was diffused through crushes on the male teachers. We vied to be teacher's pet; of course what we wanted was to be petted by them. I restricted my crushes to members of the English department. In my fantasies, we had passionate discussions after school of works of unassigned reading and my own writing. I was jealous of a female teacher who I thought was involved with the advisor for the student newspaper I edited. Years later I was informed that she was a lesbian and a classmate of mine had had an affair with her. Were we not all as innocent as I thought, or was this tale concocted for dramatic effect at our reunion?

Hunter in the early sixties was just at the cusp of the Women's Movement. The phrase hadn't yet come into use, but our school was actually a hotbed of feminism. We knew we were smart; we aspired to higher education and impressive careers. What we didn't know was how we would integrate this with the role of wife and mother, which were roles we had been raised to assume we would perform, as well. Our gallery of expectations included all those that our mothers' generation had, combined with all those our daughters' generation would have. What we didn't know, too, was how hard it would all turn out to be.

At our tenth Hunter reunion we were, for the most part, our old competitive selves. We had headed off to college and graduate school with our Hunter value system intact, and we were smug about our achievements as doctors and lawyers and college professors. By the twenty-fifth reunion we had changed, we had been softened (humanized, some would say) by the inevitable tragedies of life, as well as its pleasures. Our Hunter bond was still strong, but what united us now were the life experiences that Hunter had not prepared us for—raising children, surviving illness and divorce, dealing with the aging and death of our parents, facing our own aging, and, inevitably our own mortality, as well.

*My mother teaching biology at
Stuyvesant High School, 1965*

XIII
BIOLOGY

My mother had worked full time before I was born, and when I was a toddler she went back to teaching, in spite of my father's vigorous opposition. My father believed mothers should stay home and take care of their children; he also felt that my mother's working made it seem as if he was an insufficient provider. I don't know if he felt truly emasculated by her career, or if he was only afraid of what conservative friends and relatives would think.

A live-in nursemaid (the term "nanny" wasn't yet in fashion) took up residency in our backroom. I say nursemaid, but it would be more correct to make that plural, for one after another they left or were fired and had to be replaced. They were all young women from Iceland, fair-haired, pale-eyed and with skin so translucent white it looked like ice itself. One soon got irrevocably homesick. Another took up with a young man and closed me in my room while they made love. (I didn't know what they were up to, but my mother understood from my description of their words and sounds.) Another was irresponsible and kept losing things (although one childhood memory that prevails was of this nursemaid deliberately leaving my hand-knit sweater behind on the bench in the Oval, even after I called it to her attention, and then telling my mother it was lost. I corrected her, but who believes a two-year-old?)

Every school morning I would cry and hang on to my mother's clothes to try to keep her from going to work. Each time she left I felt she was leaving me forever. Years later, she told me she had to pry my fingers off the hem of her coat and she left for work every morning feeling sick at heart, struggling to convince herself that once she was actually gone I cheered up and had a happy day in her absence. She endured my misery, her guilt, and my father's constant disapproval, and was exhausted from managing the house, her job, and unpredictable childcare. When the latest in the series of nursemaids came down with tuberculosis, my father forced my mother to quit teaching. She stayed home for the next decade, and all of the extraordinary energy she previously put into her teaching got channeled into her role of mother. Her only offspring, I had to make up for the career she had abandoned. I was shepherded to numerous afterschool classes and activities: music, dance, art, swimming, Brownies, ice-skating. My health, my posture, my clothes, my meals, every scale I played on the violin, every book report I prepared for school was scrupulously overseen.

My mother's mother, Kaliroy, had devoted herself to her children's future, in the same spirit that my mother devoted herself to me. She always supplemented the family's income by giving Greek lessons, but her intelligence and her education were never really put to full use in a career, a commonplace for the time. She put her energies into my mother, Electra, and her younger brother, Apollo ("Appy"), and their welfare and education were her primary concerns—they always had the best clothes, toys, and books the family could afford. To make it financially possible for my mother to go to Barnard College and her brother to go to Columbia (as opposed to a public city college), her parents moved from the Bronx, where they'd lived for years, to an apartment walking distance from Columbia's campus. My mother had grown up with parental self-sacrifice as the norm, yet she had also witnessed her own mother's talents gone to waste.

When I entered junior high school, my mother finally went back to work full time. She taught biology at Stuyvesant High School (which pre-dated Stuyvesant Town and had no connection with it), fortunately a short walk from our apartment. My mother got up early in the morning, made breakfast for me and my father (who was still sleeping), made her half of the bed, and set off. From the window I could see her cutting across the Oval, heavy briefcase in one hand, pocketbook with zippered closures (the best protection against wal-let-snatchers) in the other.

Every night after she had washed and put away the dinner dishes (I dried), laid out things for breakfast the following morning (bowls upside down on the table so they wouldn't collect dust, knife laid beside the cutting board with three oranges, lined up to be sacrificed in the morning), and washed the kitchen floor, she would sit at her desk and prepare for her next day of teaching. She always had tests to correct, homework and lab reports to check over, and sev-eral different class preparations to do, including her Advanced Place-ment class, which required extra planning.

While my mother worked, my father watched T.V. in the back-room. When he got tired, he would hound my mother to go to bed, but she always had more work to do. Often he would go to sleep in the bed in the backroom while my mother toiled at her desk, in the corner of the bedroom, long past midnight. Her desk was actually the vanity table that matched the mahogany art deco bedroom set. It came with a round, backless seat that I had loved to spin on when I was little, sometimes sitting cross-legged after I had gathered enough speed with my feet, sometimes lying on my belly with my arms and legs in the arm, crying "I'm flying!" till my mother put a stop to it. My father often suggested she get herself a proper desk chair, but my mother would never spend money like that on something for herself, and she defended the austerity. She claimed the seat made her "sit up straight." When it finally succumbed to my years of spinning, she re-placed it with a straight-back wooden chair, a relic of a dining room set. It was a chair that demanded excellent posture. It neither tilted, nor swirled, and its upholstered seat was hard as wood.

When I was cleaning out the apartment after my mother's death, I found a metal filing cabinet full of stacks of her old record books from Stuyvesant High School. For every student in every class she had columns of grades (homework, lab reports, tests) and minute notations about in-class performance and extra credit work. Pages and pages of names and grades. These were the future doctors, the researchers at Rockefeller Institute, the professors at Columbia, these were the Nobel Prize winners. The future lay in her hands; their lives hinged on a single grade on a lab report that would raise or lower their class average, change their class standing, affect their chance of acceptance into Harvard or MIT. All those struggles and frustrations, boy after boy, year after year, hundreds and thousands of neat little numbers in boxes tinier than a lady bug. All their hours of labor, all her hours of labor!

I gathered the record books up in my arms. Then I carried them out into the hall and threw them all down the incinerator chute. In the old days they would have tumbled down to meet a fiery death, gone up in flames, been reduced to ashes. Now they fell into a compactor, were pressed into oblivion and carted off in a sealed container to a landfill far away.

I knew all my mother's students' names, for she talked about them at dinner every night. They were like characters in a soap opera, and they ran true to form, with few surprises. The industrious ones were always industrious; the lazy ones were always lazy. My mother was scrupulous about honesty and if she suspected someone of cheating, she would lay a trap where they would be caught. If she suspected someone copied answers on exams, she would make up a special exam for him so his neighbor's answers would be all wrong. If two students were suspected of illegal collaboration, she would get them to turn each other in, and then expose their disloyalty along with their dishonesty. No one ever cheated twice in her class, and probably never again in Stuyvesant High School, but my mother was not optimistic about human nature. She held great store in genes and the influence of early environment. By the time her students got to her, she felt, their characters were already formed for life. In spite of this, she labored to get each student to make the best of himself and blamed herself when he didn't. She had special affection for bright losers—a kid who sparkled with genius but couldn't discipline himself. These were the students who most inspired her, and often she inspired them.

There were always boys who hung around my mother after school. Sometimes they followed her home, as if she were the pied piper, sometimes right upstairs to our apartment, where they would be enthralled by drosophila breeding in jars on our window sills, or pester her with questions about the latest issue of *Scientific American*. Stuyvesant High School boys were more notable for their brains than their looks, and my mother's sycophants were a particularly be-spectacled, bepimpled bunch. Still, Hunter girls, in their all-female sanctuary, could not be choosy. Every girl at Hunter longed for some connection with Stuyvesant High School. And here I lived with one, and nothing came of it at all. The boys I knew through my mother either ignored me or looked upon me as a pal. Even the few who considered dating at all never asked me out.

The two mixers I attended with Stuyvesant High School were disasters. At one, a boy asked me if I was Mrs. Demas's daughter, and when I confessed I was he informed me that he, and everyone else, thought she had named her daughter Chlorine. Another boy dropped my hands and abandoned me on the dance floor when my identity was revealed. "I know your mother," he said. "She failed me."

It would be of no surprise to anyone that I was a mediocre science student. I despised chemistry and got the lowest grade in my high school career in it. I was squeamish in biology lab. I could not pith a frog and felt so dizzy at the sight of the dead creatures I had to go in the hall. The odor of formaldehyde made me nauseated. Some of the photographs in my biology textbook upset me so much I had to paperclip them closed so I wouldn't open to them by accident.

I pretended indifference to the subject of biology, as much as possible, but my mother's enthusiasm made it difficult. She always had a microscope out, was always discovering something interesting to show me. Her own delight was contagious, however I fought it.

"What is life?"

My mother posed the question to me at the dinner table. I was around twelve and hadn't taken biology in school yet.

Things were alive when they grew, or changed, or moved on their own, I suggested.

My mother did her introductory classroom demonstration for me. She took a piece of shiny paper, crumpled it up and set it on the table. It popped into life, exploding open, making noise, moving entirely on its own.

"Is this alive?" she asked.

And it certainly seemed so, this paper creature that expanded so energetically, crackled, flipped.

But life wasn't that simple. The answer would take a whole year of study, a survey of the definition: "A series of complex functions such as metabolism, growth, response to stimuli, and reproduction." The definition was a tautology. Life was—life. You would be sure when it wasn't there, and sure when it was, but there would be all that stuff in the middle that you wouldn't be so sure about. It was easy to call the dog alive and the glass paperweight not. But what about the lichens on the trees and the mold on the bathroom shower curtain? What about the tulip bulb before it was planted in the ground, before the emergence of its first wedge of green?

And even my mother, with all her years of teaching about it, and all her brilliance, could only define life and recognize it. She could not explain for me *why* it was—how it had happened, and what there was before and after it. Nor could she explain death.

Reproduction, however she could explain, and she did. She explained it to me, and she explained it to scores of Stuyvesant High School boys, the very boys whom I would face at mixers. The way my mother talked about reproduction, however, it had nothing at all to do with sex. No one in her class sniggered when she talked about testes and ovaries any more than they did when she talked about mitochondria or planaria. Cells were cells. Reproductive organs were reproductive organs.

I wonder how many young men, former Stuyvesant High

School boys (few had much experience with girls when they were still at Stuyvesant) in the midst of arduous groping suddenly pictured cross sections of the male and female reproductive system, heard in their minds my mother's voice describing the egg's noble journey down the fallopian tubes, and found their ardor cooled. Perhaps my mother's lectures on reproduction and on birth control were, in themselves, the best form of birth control.

In spite of the proof of my own nonvirgin birth, it was hard for me to imagine that my mother had ever abandoned herself to the frivolities of sex, that she had indulged in something that by her standards for human activity was so obviously a waste of time. Yet there was no other way to explain my parents' marriage. In spite of antithetical temperaments, attitudes, tastes, and interests, and in spite of the fact they were constantly exasperated with each other, they were fiercely attracted to each other, too. If my mother were still alive, reading over my shoulder now she would laugh and tell me I should note the power of preservation of the species.

And so I have.

My mother believed that women were smarter than men, but they had to pretend not to be. She believed that women ultimately held all the power, but they exercised that power through manipulation, rather than overt force. Men's egos were fragile things, and women had to conspire to keep them intact. You flattered men, humored men, made much of their supposed virility. You did it for your own self-interest: men performed better sexually, therefore serviced women's pleasure better, if they felt good about themselves. Of course women were superior because, biologically, men were unnecessary. Men were merely sperm donors, and could otherwise be eliminated from the life process. It was women's job to keep them from feeling quite as useless as they were. And so they let them drive the family car and sit at the head of the table and carve the roast, and let them believe they made all the decisions.

The basic flaw in my mother's schema was her acceptance of

the traditional view that all the domestic labor, therefore, fell to women. In our house my mother did everything related to the maintenance of life. She made all social arrangements. She planned all vacations. She was entirely in charge of rearing me. My father would have been hard pressed to remember the name of my teacher or what grade I was in. He was entirely oblivious to my school day, whereas my mother knew it minute by minute. He had little idea about my afterschool activities. The names of my friends were a blur. It wasn't that my father loved me any less, it's that my mother was as involved in my life as she was in her own. My father wasn't.

When my mother had been a full-time homemaker, all domestic duties fell to her naturally enough. When she resumed her full-time job, however, the division of labor didn't change. When I was old enough to question the inequity of this, her excuse was that my father had a "harder job" or a "longer working day," or, most simply that he was a man. My mother never complained directly, though she sometimes wore the look of a martyr. If she ever wanted a hand with the chores, it was me she turned to, never my father. On the few occasions when he had attempted to perform one of my mother's regular household tasks, he did such an inferior job she never allowed him to do it again. She had no tolerance for an imperfectly scrubbed bathtub or a bed made with the spread pulled straight across the pillows instead of tucked in tight along the front. It would have been impossible for anyone to meet her exacting standards, and my father had little incentive to try. He cultivated incompetence because it protected him from having to work, and he was abetted by my mother's complicity. On one occasion I prodded him into making dinner; he broiled the steak without removing it first from its plastic wrapping.

Only my mother's death cured my father's domestic ineptitude. In his eighties, now, living on his own, he does a fine job of maintaining himself and his home. Though he relies on the toaster oven rather than the real stove, and the dust buster rather than the vacuum cleaner, my mother would be astonished how much he learned from her, without ever letting on.

XIV

WOMAN'S WORK

It was with considerable reluctance that my mother was driven to employ a cleaning woman when she resumed teaching full time. Her ethic dictated that each person maintain her own spot on the earth (though mothers were responsible for the maintenance of everyone in their family) and it troubled her on a fundamental level to have some other woman, a woman less fortunate than she, toiling on her behalf. Since she would no more compromise her standards of cleanliness and order than she would her preparedness for teaching, there was no alternative to hiring someone to help out with her domestic duties. She assuaged her conscience by always working while her cleaning woman worked. Either she was at school teaching, or she was in the apartment performing another—preferably more unpleasant—household chore.

Mrs. Gibson was an anomaly among cleaning women. Other families in Stuyvesant Town hired robust immigrants from Haiti or the Dominican Republic, or black women from Harlem. They all went by their first names. If Mrs. Gibson had a first name, I never knew it. She was white, thin, frail, and furtive. She had a perpetual cough. She was certainly older than my mother, but probably not as old as she looked. Her eyes were watery blue and her baby-fine hair, shoulder length, might once have been auburn. She wore a green uniform, which smelled of cigarettes, perfume past its prime, and sweat, though she moved so slowly while she worked it must have been sweat leftover from another time in her life. It was amazing she was alive at all, for she hardly ate, her lungs were in terrible shape from smoking, and I knew from conversations overheard between my parents that she was an alcoholic.

Mrs. Gibson had had a tragic life, of that I was certain, though the facts were hazy. What I knew was that she lived in a room in the Hotel Chelsea, on West Twenty-third Street, and that she had a wealthy nephew who gave her expensive presents—an alligator pocketbook, opera glasses—and every year sent her on a lavish cruise or winter vacation in the Bahamas. We got postcards to prove it, and sometimes she'd bring me back souvenirs. The story was either she had come from a well-to-do family and been "cut off" when she had married someone whom they disapproved of, or she had married a man from a well-to-do family who didn't approve of her, and had been left penniless at his death. The possibility that she may not actually have been married didn't occur to me till I started writing about her. It was certainly not a possibility that would have been broached in the chaste world of Stuyvesant Town. In any case, her working as a maid was a secret, scrupulously guarded from the benevolent nephew.

"But if he knew she had to work as a maid, wouldn't he help support her?" I asked.

"She'd never let him know," my mother answered.

"Why not?"

My mother had a simple, one word answer, a word that elevated Mrs. Gibson forever in my mind. "Pride," she said.

Mrs. Gibson flicked at the dust on the bookcases with a dust rag (my old pajama top) moist with furniture polish. She wearily dragged the vacuum cleaner from room to room. She halfheartedly ran the mop across the kitchen and bathroom floor. But when it came to ironing she was an artist. It was for that, no doubt, that my mother hired her. For in addition to the quantity of unpressed clothes that any Stuyvesant Town family would generate each week, there were my father's dental "gowns"—white, short-sleeved uniforms with snaps that ran up the side and across the shoulder. They had to be perfectly done, for they were symbols of my father's professionalism, his impeccable sanitary standards.

The ironing board was set up in the backroom and the bed there was piled with the newly washed, wrinkled clothes awaiting Mrs. Gibson's touch. By the end of the afternoon the bed was empty and the closet rack was lined with garments that had been transformed.

Mrs. Gibson would lay out a blouse tenderly on the ironing board. She divided it into territories: front, back, sleeves, collar, and concentrated on each one in turn. The iron had to be just hot enough to make the fibers submit to flatness, but not too hot and scorch. She used the pointed tip of the iron to nose into the crevices between tucks and to outline the territory around buttons, the wide flat of the iron for the larger expanses of cloth. She knew when to let the iron glide, when to let it linger, when to work with it smooth and dry, when to let loose a great hiss of steam,

When she was done she'd hang up the blouse and button all the buttons. It could barely be recognized as the same, misshapen bit of cloth it had been just a short while before. It had crispness, shape, and even stature that it didn't have when it was brand new. Even though it was just hanging there, it seemed something more than a mere blouse; it had three-dimensionality, a life of its own.

Eventually Mrs. Gibson stopped working for us. She stopped working altogether. If, old and ill, she finally succumbed, abandoned pride and fell on the mercy of her nephew, or if she spent her last months supported by the generosity of the state, we never heard.

Mrs. Gibson was succeeded by Daisy, who worked for neighbors on Eleven. Daisy's life was hard, but in a way quite unlike Mrs. Gibson's. She was the head of a large, extended family, and had no time to be melancholy. She was never alone. She took care of her children, her grandchildren, her elders. Every week she'd leave our apartment, laden with shopping bags of old clothes, toys, and household articles—my mother would gather them from neighbors—which she distributed among the needy in her Harlem neighborhood. My mother was always careful to make sure that anything to be recycled was clean and in good condition. Once Daisy had shown my mother a battered hat that another employer had passed onto her that morning. Daisy modeled it for my mother, laughing.

"Can you imagine, Mrs. Demas, she expects folks like us would wear a hat like this!"

Though Daisy wanted my mother to call her by her first name, it was inconceivable to her that she would call my mother Electra.

Daisy climbed up on the stepstool and vacuumed the tops of the drapes, she chased down the dustballs under the beds, she scrubbed the kitchen floor on her hands and knees. But ironing was just a job to her, like any other. Some blouses retained a few wrinkles. Some suffered scorch spots. But soon enough permanent press clothing—a new invention—took over our wardrobes, and ironing didn't matter much anymore.

In Stuyvesant Town today, there's a laundry room on the main floor of our building, a corner relinquished by the old carriage room. When I was a child, there was a central laundry room for several buildings, and getting the laundry done required a trip outdoors. A week's worth of dirty laundry barely squeezed into my mother's shopping cart.

The laundry room was a steamy, noisy place, run by women in white uniforms. They kept order, made change, did the laundry for residents who were willing to pay for such a luxury, and mopped up the floods when washing machines overflowed, which was a regular occurrence. Too much soap powder and the bubbles built up beyond capacity and started frothing out of a funnel at the top of the machine, like a pot boiling over. My mother would never be guilty of causing such a cataract, but I had been fortunate enough to be on the premises for several dramatic ones. Through the porthole window of the machine you could anticipate the coming danger: the bubbles germinated and multiplied, and soon the window was opaque with whiteness. It was a like a great wave breaking on shore, but the water was hot and you had to dash to safety.

An intermediary between the washing machine and the dryer was the extractor, a machine that spun the clothes dizzy and sucked out enough water so the clothes were primed for the dryer. It was a dryer big enough for a child to sit inside of, though no worse sin could be imagined than climbing inside one (except perhaps hiding in an abandoned refrigerator, in the unlikely case that one presented itself).

Sometimes women would put their wash in the dryer, go off on an errand and not return to claim their clothes before the dryer stopped. In such cases, if you were waiting for a dryer, it was considered perfectly ethical to remove those clothes and dump them into a laundry cart. It was an odd feeling to scoop out a stranger's clothing, warm and staticky from the dryer, to see their pajamas and underpants. My mother certainly didn't want some stranger handling our undergarments, so she was always on hand when the dryer came to its final stop.

Men were allowed in the laundry room, but they trespassed so rarely it was possible to surmise that they weren't. There were no widowers or bachelors living in Stuyvesant Town in those days, and certainly no single fathers. Fathers braved the laundry room only when their wives were seriously incapacitated, and the laundry room ladies usually ran to their rescue—for left to manage on their own they would no doubt flood the machines or mix the coloreds with the whites.

Bedsheets, tablecloths, cloth napkins, and my father's shirts went to the Chinese laundry on First Avenue. My mother changed our beds every week, and that first night the sheets were so smooth I was afraid to crease them in my sleep. They were what cleanliness smelled like. My mother dropped off the dirty shirts and linens in a laundry bag. When she picked them up they were folded, stacked, wrapped in brown paper, and tied with string, the laundry bag on the top of the pile, bleached and pressed as if it were fine linen.

My father's shirts were folded around a rectangle of cardboard, and these shirt cardboards were collected in the bottom of my father's drawer. They were an indispensable constant of my childhood. I used them for report covers, to tape my leaf collections to, for dioramas. When my father took Spanish lessons (so that he could converse with the increasing number of Puerto Rican patients), they were propped up all around the bathroom, with his Spanish vocabulary words and conjugated verbs.

A favorite ritual in my childhood was the defrosting of the re-frigerator. The refrigerator provided for us by Stuyvesant Town was a one-door model with the ice-box (as my mother still called the freezer compartment) a small metal vault inside, flanked by shelves for bottles of milk. It was not frost free. Defrosting it was, indisputably, woman's work. One Stuyvesant Town wife who asked her husband to perform the task while she went shopping, returned home to discover he had simply unplugged the refrigerator, and left it to its own devices. My mother never even asked my father.

I emptied the refrigerator and my mother placed pots of boiling water on the shelves inside. The ice trays, in a strange reversal of their duties, were filled with hot water and slid back into their slot. The great thaw began. It was like a blast of summer in the middle of January. Slabs of ice on the freezer box lost their hold and fell into the waiting meat tray below. It was a war between hot and cold, and hot always won. It was not exactly a fair fight, because my mother would replace lukewarm pots of water with freshly boiled ones, and whittle off particularly stubborn ice chunks with a spatula. When the ice was conquered, my mother removed all the metal shelves and washed them in hot soapy water. I washed the great, emptied interior with baking soda. The sponge squealed across that sleek, enamel surface. I always remembered the cautionary tale of a child who had played in an empty refrigerator, and been locked inside when the door had slammed shut. I imagined the terror of that absolute darkness, sound-proof, lightproof, airtight.

When the refrigerator had been completely dried inside with fresh dishcloths (castoff linen towels from my father's office), the shelves were replaced. I wiped off each jar and container before placing it back on the shelves. Every bead of moisture had to be swabbed dry, for moisture instantly turned into ice and hastened the time to the next defrosting.

In more recent years, when Stuyvesant Town updated the original refrigerator with a new frost-free model, my mother still regularly cleaned out the refrigerator. She did not miss the arduousness of ice-removal, but she did express concern that the frost-free versions allowed a lowering of hygiene in the population at large. There were women now—she was sure of it (in fact her own daughter confesses to being one) who never emptied and thoroughly cleaned their refrigerators at all.

The only domestic task that fell upon my father with any regularity, was taking out the garbage. The incinerator was in the hall by the elevators. You stuffed your bag of garbage inside the depository, and pushed it closed, as if you were mailing a package. The air was dense with soot, and inevitably you got smudges on your sleeve. The garbage tumbled through black space and landed in a pile at the bottom of the shaft, where it was incinerated, mingled with and indistinguishable from your neighbors'. The ash was shoveled into metal garbage cans, which were lined up along the street, then dumped into a garbage truck, then dumped into barges on the East River and towed out and dumped at sea. There's no incinerator anymore. Today the garbage is compacted, then shipped off, untouched, untransformed by fire.

A notice on the incinerator door warned you about what could not be discarded, but even the most law-abiding souls tended to ignore the rules. Things that didn't fit down the chute (like a broken chair), or things that people thought their neighbors might use (like old books or magazines) were left by the incinerator door. Anything you didn't want to be traced to you, you stripped of identifying labels and left off on another floor, usually taking the stairs by night. Not everyone was so scrupulous. From a pile of magazines by the incinerator door, I once rescued a Metropolitan Museum engagement book, where a hapless neighbor had forgotten she had recorded her menstrual cycle.

Scrounging was a devious art. No one wanted to be caught in the act, so people darted out to the hall when the coast was clear, and ducked back into their apartments if they heard anyone come. Garbage hounds, like my father, would ride the elevators up and down at night, checking out the discards on other floors. When he would bring home in triumph a perfectly good toaster (that needed only a new cord) that he had salvaged on Six, my mother would make him cart it right out again. Sometimes he snuck things into the house, and tried repairing them in secret in the backroom.

The janitor, Hippoleto, went through the building every morning and gathered the remains of the discards. His little room on the main floor was a storehouse of things he had salvaged for himself, an archeological sampling of the lives of 524 East Twentieth Street. It was the kind of hide-out my father would consider heaven: a sagging sofa you could stretch out on and smoke a cigar, a scarred coffee table you could put your feet up on, and two television sets, side by side, one with no picture the other with no sound.

The Howdy Doody Show, 1950

XV

TELEVISION

When our first television came into our apartment, when I was around five, my mother decided it belonged not in the living room, but in the backroom, the room that became my father's lair. It was a large piece of mahogany furniture and it was placed beside the window, with the spire of the Empire State Building in the distant view pointing up above its shoulder. There was something about the concept of television—perhaps the indolence of it—that bothered my mother fundamentally. She assuaged her qualms by not providing a comfortable viewing situation. We either sat on straightback chairs or on the bed, and leaned against the hard wall. It was several years before my father rebelled and carted off to the backroom a comfortable livingroom chair.

It was a black and white world, that world of the Fifties, the shows on television, the photographs in the album. As soon as you tried to seize or copy reality, the color drained right out of it. Years later when I saw my first color television I was dazzled. How dull black and white seemed in comparison, yet we had been so awed by early television we'd never noticed its flaw. As a young child it never occurred to me that the characters on *Leave It To Beaver* or *Father Knows Best* existed in a world of color like mine. I thought of them as grey families in a grey world.

The Howdy Doody Show was a mainstay of my early childhood. I was frightened by Clarabelle, that voiceless, honking clown, but entranced by Princess Summerfallwinterspring, especially when I decoded her name. When it was Howdy Doody time, television sets all over Stuyvesant Town clicked on. I could look out the backroom window and catch glimpses of Howdy's wooden grin in apartments catty-corner and below ours, or legs or backs of children in their televisions' glow. Through the Gleasons, neighbors who worked in television, every child in 524 had the opportunity to be on *The Howdy Doody Show* in the Peanut Gallery. This major achievement of my early years was immortalized in a photo, black and white, of course. Alas, the Gleasons' power didn't extend to Walt Disney Enterprises and I spent the next few years of my life longing for a chance to be on *The Mickey Mouse Club*. There was no child in Stuyvesant Town, no child in my class, who wasn't under its spell. It was an assumption of our common experience, and children whose families didn't own televisions gathered to watch regularly in the homes of those who did. Though Annette and Darlene were heavy favorites of my friends, I was a fan of Karen, the smallest girl. I say "fans," but in fact we did not truly like these child actresses; we were consumed by jealousy of them. We all wanted to be Mousketeers, ourselves. In our bedrooms, secretly, we tilted our faces and sang the Mickey Mouse Club song. Maybe some unseen producer would magically hear us, and pluck us up out of anonymity and put us on the show.

Ironically I came to be elevated to the glory of radio and television not because of performance abilities, but because of bookishness. I worked as a volunteer in Hunter's school library during my study hall, shelving books and stamping cards. It was the librarian, pink-cheeked, powdered Miss Tilley, her hair in a librarian's requisite wispy bun, who recommended her prodigies for a program produced by the New York Public Library, called "Young Book Reviewers." In the early years this panel discussion aired on WMCA, and followed a popular radio show hosted by a man named Barry Gray, selected, no doubt for his rhyming name. The studio was a windowless, sealed box, with air so refined of any sound of the city or of nature—wind or rain or bird twitter—we could have been in an orbiting spacecraft. We sported large buttons that said "WMCA Young Book Reviews" with window slots for our names so we could be called on during show time. On radio you were invisible, as were all kinds of visual clues and signals: pinched fingers pulling apart imaginary taffy meant "stretch it out"; a forefinger drawn across the neck meant "cut."

We panelists sat on both sides of a long banquet table, with the moderator, Margaret C. Scoggin, at the head, and the author at her side. There was no food, only little glasses of water, and headphones and a mike for each of us. At the beginning of the show we introduced ourselves and named the school we were representing. One of the chief tasks was to suppress giggles, a condition adolescent girls are particularly prone to. The inclination to giggle was aggravated by Miss Scoggin's opening "good morning," which invariably sounded as severe as a newscaster about to announce a major disaster. Off duty, my friends on the show and I could reduce each other to fits of laughter by imitating her opening. At actual show time we kept our eyes low, chins tucked down, and gripped the edge of our chairs. One time I lost control and dashed from the studio, ripping wires in my wake, and slammed into Barry Gray in the corridor. The mortifying thought that everyone assumed I'd had a bathroom emergency was a quick antidote to laughter, and I returned to my spot on the panel, chastened and grim, though careful to avoid eye contact with any of my friends.

After its stint on WMCA, "Young Book Reviewers" moved to a more fitting home, the public radio station WNYC, "The Voice of New York," and the tapings were done in the Donnell Library. When we got older, perhaps at the instigation of a smart PR person, its name was changed to "Teenage Book Talk," though not even the catchiest title could alter the fact that this was not a show likely to catch anyone's fancy. The show was taped on Friday afternoon and aired on Saturday morning. I am sure no one listened to it except the proud families of the panelists, and perhaps a few unfortunate children whose parents thought it educational fare. I listened to myself on a transistor radio in the lunchroom of Third Street Music School, while my parents, at home, faithfully taped each show on their reel-to-reel tape recorder. The thrill of being on the radio was always off-set by the agony I experienced hearing my voice, which sounded like a little boy's.

The guest authors on the program included the famous—Bennet Cerf, Ogden Nash, Eleanor Roosevelt—and the unknown. I am sure the authors came out of a certain civic duty rather than any hope that the show would boost sales. The books, though brand new, were the property of the New York Public library, lent to us for the week, so I collected autographs on the program sheet. To add to my thrill of meeting Eleanor Roosevelt, I was the one who got to escort her out of the building after the show. In the elevator going down she put on her gloves and I noticed there was a hole at the tip of one finger. A limousine waited for her outside, but until she stepped into its dark interior, she was indistinguishable from any of the ordinary patrons of the library.

On several occasions I was selected from the radio panel to be on a television cousin, called "Reading Is Fun." What was fun was to be excused from school early, to be in a television studio instead of suffering the inquiries of the French teacher about some subtlety of the subjunctive. I had to remember not to wear white (it makes you look dead) or stripes (they go all zig-zag). A makeup person dusted my face with a powder to reduce the shine. On television everything was exposed. The camera wasn't on you at all times, but you never knew when it might be. You had to keep your back straight and your knees together. You could not shut your eyes and crimp your lips together to suppress giggles. Most important, you had to avoid the temptation to watch the monitor, though it was the only chance to see yourself on the screen. There were no home videos then, no way to see the show later. To be on television gave me a sensation of more than fame—it was like a brush with immortality. That was your voice, your image, floating on that magical current, multiplying itself in countless televisions across the country. You were suddenly, instantly in rooms you had never seen, in places you had never been.

When I was on television, my father took time off between patients and went down to the appliance store near his office, where the owner obliged by turning on the proper channel of every television in the place, and the half dozen in the window. All pedestrians passing along that block of Seventh Avenue got to see a snippet of "Reading Is Fun," while my father joyfully pointed out to every customer in the place the face on the screen that was his kid.

XVI

GREEKS

To be Greek was to be a lifelong member of a secret club, to have kinship with otherwise total strangers. When Greek-Americans ran into each other, especially in a part of the country remote from Greek communities, there was an immediate sense of camaraderie, of family. I was certainly a member of a minority group. We were the only Greeks in our apartment building, among the few in Stuyvesant Town. I was the only child of Greek descent at Hunter Elementary School, one of two in my class in high school.

There weren't enough Greek immigrants in America to make themselves unpopular. They didn't steal jobs from the natives; they merely added restaurants. Their names usually gave them away. Perfectly dignified grownups had multisyllabic names that ended in a string of "opolises," ridiculous to a child's ear. The name Demas was recognized by all Greeks as Greek, but non-Greeks often guessed that it was French, and pronounced it that way. I could pass as anything I wanted. Most often people assumed I was Jewish.

Some people connect modern Greeks with their classical heritage (a link that Greeks, themselves, assume with pride). Americans far from the places where Greek immigrants have clustered—like Astoria, New York, Manchester, N.H., and Naples, Florida—might find a Greek as exotic as Odysseus himself. Greeks are caricatured as dark, oily, jovial, musical, plump, industrious, and sexually active. Most Greeks who immigrated to America came from the southern part of Greece, the Peloponnesus, where dark eyes and hair were, in fact, prevalent. My father's family came from Sparta, in the south. My mother's family came from the north of Greece where blue eyes are common and children are often blond.

My maternal grandfather, Constantine Athanasius Guizot, ("*Guizotis*" in Greek) was lean and wiry with a long, bumpy nose that would have been a disaster on a woman's face. He had pale eyelashes, like a child's, and eyes that changed color like those mood rings that were popular when I was a teenager, depending on the color of his shirt—green, blue, grey. Hazel was what he wrote on his driver's license.

My grandfather had traveled to Athens from his village in Macedonia to go the university, but found himself about to be drafted for the Greek army, instead, and hopped on a ship to America. He headed to Brockton, Massachusetts, where he had a cousin, and started a newspaper for the Greek community there, called the *Chronos* ("Times"), an alternative to working, as many Greeks did, in the shoe factories. He was the publisher, editor, advertising manager, and, at times, the entire staff.

My mother's mother, Kaliroy Wolf ("*Volfis*" in Greek), came from Yannina, a city on the West of Greece, where her father owned a coach business between there and the port city of Preveza. She came to America to escape the tyranny of her stepmother, and lived with family friends. She got a job working on the *Atlantis,* the Greek newspaper in New York.

When my grandmother met my grandfather and fell in love she wrote to her father that she was planning to get married. He immediately came over (or as immediately as one could when it involved many days journey to Athens and as many days journey across the sea). He found the apartment in New York where my grandmother was living, and since she was not home, left his calling card with a note, and went out to see the city, returning at dinner time to his astonished daughter. He did not approve of the young man she had chosen—thought him unlikely to make a success of himself—and to prove this to his daughter, he decided to demonstrate what, by contrast, an ambitious man might do. He bought work clothes in bulk in the city, traveled out west selling them at a profit to the workers along the expanding railroad, and came back to show his daughter how much money he had made in such a short time. My existence is entirely owing to the fact that her romantic nature won out over her good sense and filial duty.

In the end, my great grandfather was right about his son-in-law, at least he was right that he had no great business sense. After the newspaper my grandfather had a succession of enterprises, including a chain of movie houses, a restaurant, and a radio and electric appliance store (which, in all fairness to his business acumen, was a victim of the Crash). By the time I was born he had settled on a double career—working for the U.S. Post Office (where he was head of the Dead Letter Department) and being an accountant (he did the books of Greek restaurants and florists). He never did get a university degree, but he saw that his children did. He didn't think of himself as an intellectual, but he would read Plato and Sophocles in Ancient Greek for pleasure, amuse himself learning French, and in his eighties started teaching himself Chinese for a trip to China.

My ability to speak Greek was minimal, but I understood a considerable amount. My parents spoke Greek in my presence when they didn't want me to know what they were talking about, and then, illogically, spoke Greek to me in public, when they didn't want other people to know what they were saying. Greek was a perfect secret language. My mother, who had opinions about everything and everyone she laid on eyes on, used Greek in situations when she wanted to tell me something privately. In Greek, she would say out loud in public what she couldn't possibly say in English. She would give nothing away with her face, often smiling while she condemned. She used Greek to remind me about my posture, to tell me to modulate my voice, to stop picking at a scab, or a whatever else I did that was a breach of manners or a threat to my health or welfare.

At times I was embarrassed by the Greek; I didn't want people to think I was a foreigner. At times I delighted in our subterfuge. My mother's audacity was remarkable. She would talk about people who were sitting next to us, speculate about relationships, comment on their clothing and their conversation, while she pretended she wasn't talking about them at all. It was as if we had a cloak of invisibility. At a restaurant, with the waiter hovering over us, she would tell me not to select things on the menu that might not be fresh. In front of the saleswoman in the girl's department of Altman's my mother would tell me she'd seen the same velvet dress I wanted for half the price at Orbach's. On the Lexington Avenue bus she would point out a girl sitting across from us who didn't have her knees together and the man across the aisle could look up her skirt.

A few times we overheard other Greeks conversing in public much as we did, with the same arrogance that they could not be understood by anyone around them. We'd lie silent in conspiracy, listening to their private conversation, and smiling over it. It was a trick I delighted in, this eavesdropping on Greeks—sometimes we would reveal ourselves, sometimes not.

One summer, driving through Florida, my parents had miscalculated the distance to the next town where they had hoped to reach a restaurant by dinner time. It was dark, it was the Everglades, and we were all hungry. I, expert whiner, had been "starving" for hours. Finally we came upon a small restaurant by the roadside in the middle of nowhere. It didn't look open and there were no cars in the parking lot, but my father banged on the door anyway until the owner emerged. He was very sorry, he said, but they had already closed. My father pleaded with him, for "sandwiches, anything!" pointing back to the car where I and my mother gazed out anxiously.

The man, shook his head with regret. The kitchen had been closed up for the night. He was on his way home.

My father cried out the worst Greek curse I knew, "*istothiavalo,*" which means "go to the devil." Under ordinary circumstances, these were fighting words to any Greek. But these were not ordinary circumstances.

The restaurant owner's face lit up *"Hellenes?"* "Greeks?" he cried out. Here in the most godforsaken spot in the dark of Florida he had discovered a compatriot. The restaurant was miraculously opened up, the lights all went on, the restaurant owner's wife, mother, and children came out from their house behind the restaurant. The kitchen was brought to life, the best table was set. We feasted and drank and shared histories, and the only thing that threatened the bonhomie was when the restaurant owner was insulted when my father attempted to pay for the meal.

That was a defining episode of my childhood. I discovered I was a member of an underground sect. I could reveal my Greek identity, like a Mason showing his ring, in times of need, and I could count on Greeks rescuing Greeks. And in turn, I would look out for other Greeks, befriend and support them when I could.

Greek-American politicians make the most of this. My parents held out against Spiro Agnew, but many Greeks we knew voted for him, even though they didn't like him, even though it meant voting Republican for the first and only time in their lives. No wonder the frenzy when Greeks had Democrats they could take pleasure in voting for, like Dukakis or Tsongas.

There was always a close connection between being Greek and being Greek Orthodox. It was like being Jewish, both an ethnic and a religious thing. There was no cultural center for Greek atheists. They had to make their way in the land of vague Protestants, in the land of all the other atheists, their ethnic heritage bleached out.

For a short time in my childhood, my father would take me off with him on Sunday mornings to the small Greek Orthodox Church in Brooklyn his mother attended, and where I as a baby, though screaming in protest, had been dunked in holy water and officially baptized. My mother never joined us. I would leave her working for her Monday classes, her desk covered with piles of student papers.

In the front of the church there was a stand with an icon, under a plate of glass. People kissed this as they entered, as they would kiss a relative when they entered their home. The glass had smudges of lipstick and saliva on it. My mother said I should bend, as if kissing, but never let my lips touch. Just as you might kiss a corpse at a wake. I bent my head and kept my lips pinched. I came within an inch of the glass, no closer, and held my breath against germs.

At a long table with a tray filled with sand you dropped money in the collection box and took small, flesh-colored candles and stuck them in sand. You lit one for each dead person you wanted to remember. The flames were like little faces at the top of armless, one-legged bodies. The souls were alive for as long as the candle lasted, which wasn't very long. The wax dripped down on the sand, the candle was soon a stump. It seemed to me better never to invoke the soul at all, than to bring it there for such a brief life and then abandon it to its certain fate.

I sat with my father in the church, but only old women occupied the front pews, and most of the men stood against the pews along the walls. The music was always mournful, nothing in a major key, and few tunes. Even the priests who could not sing, did so, unembarrassed by their quavering, unmusical voices, the wails of animals. When the priest walked down the aisle, swinging his censer, I turned my face from the cloud of incense. The smell awakened all my fears, like the smell of alcohol in a doctor's office. I didn't know the rituals; I was on stage, for a play I hadn't rehearsed. Once, by mistake I ended up sitting in a row that filed up in front to take communion. I could not escape. I copied the girl ahead of me, took a piece of bread, kissed a ringed hand. These acts had no more connection to God for me, than passing through the checkout line at D'Agostino's. Knowing this, knowing I was an imposter, filled me with terror. What did this church do to children who did not believe?

The second religious experiment was the Greek Orthodox Cathedral in Manhattan, a larger, more prosperous church, where my parents had been married, and where my father had gone to Greek school as a child. Full-sized icons stood across the front of the church, the saints' features flat as paper dolls. I was sent to join the Sunday school class where I shocked the teacher with my sacrilegious notions, my mother's scientific explanations for the miracles of the Bible. I was told that I had to believe in miracles, that it was an act of faith.

How can you be forced to believe something? Belief was like love. You could not learn it, or be converted to it, it happened inside you, all on its own. My mother, when confronted with my dilemma, got around it all by saying she believed in science, that it was a form of religion, that everything had its equivalents. She'd reduced it to a semantic game. I never asked my father if he actually believed in religion. I was afraid he might. His mother made the sign of the cross over her body as if she believed it all. I said nothing to her at all.

My Grandpa Guizot, without any attempt at delicacy, pronounced the whole thing nonsense. Church was for the ignorant and the old widows who had nothing better to do, he told me, I was too smart for it.

I wasn't very old when church was abandoned. My father slept late on Sunday mornings. My mother continued working at her lesson plans. When my father got up he went to the newsstand for the Sunday *New York Times* and the bakery for coffee cake. My father read the sports section of the paper, my mother read the book review, and they took turns picking at the crossword puzzle. God and Christ were mentioned no more than some tenants of our building who had once lived on the third floor and moved away.

In spite of all the evidence against it, there was part of me that always believed I was really Jewish. Even my friends who knew I wasn't, often forgot. I was assured that I "looked Jewish," that I could pass. My non-Jewish classmates were obviously so—Chinese or Black, and my friend Barbara who had freckles, red hair, and an Irish last name. Once at the high school lunch table a girl started telling a joke about Jesus Christ, then noticed me and suddenly stopped.

"It's all right," said a friend, looking at me, "She's one of us."

Of course it was all right. I was shocked to think that anyone would imagine that just because my ancestors were vaguely Christian I might take offense. When I was younger, at a Stuyvesant Town

Chanukah celebration, I was asked by another child if I was Jewish. "Half Jewish," I remember saying, since that seemed like a safer lie. I knew that neither of my parents was Jewish, but somewhere, I felt, there must have been a link. If nothing else, I felt myself to be at least an honorary Jew. I was actually a second-generation honorary Jew. My mother was the only non-Jew among her friends at Barnard College, and those three women—Leonore, Eleanor, Miriam—along with her postcollege friend Ruth, were my surrogate Jewish aunts.

I joined my neighbors in lighting their menorah, and some of my Christmas presents were funneled through their house for Chanukah. I loved lox and bagels, I could dance the horah, I could play the dreidel game. Like my Jewish friends I was haunted by images from *The Diary of Anne Frank* and Leon Uris' *Exodus* (which I could bear to read only part of). I fantasized hiding out in the attic of my grandfather's house in the country. There was no doubt in my mind that when the Nazis went after their victims, I, too, would have been rounded up.

I didn't go to any christenings when I was growing up, but I did attend lots of bar mitzvahs. At one I was the partner of the bar mitzvah himself. At the reception in a hotel ballroom the band leader announced the names of the couples as we walked across the vast polished floor to the banquet table. I felt like royalty. Later, an old lady took me aside and asked me which temple I went to. When I confessed that I didn't, she tut-tutted me and said, "For shame, a nice Jewish girl like you!" For the rest of the evening I worried that I would be found out. The parents of my friend might be open-minded enough to allow their son to pair off with a shiksa at his bar mitzvah, I thought, but the elderly relatives might take their canes to me. It wasn't until years later I realized that I had been suffering the same insecurity my Jewish friends experienced in situations where they were afraid Jews were unwelcome.

When I left New York to attend college in New England, I discovered how unusual the world I had grown up in really was. I would assume people were Jewish when they weren't. I was incredulous when someone named Schwartz or Zimmerman said they weren't Jewish. What was equally surprising was their indignation that I mistook them for Jews. I remember someone apologizing to me because they had thought I was Jewish, then discovered I wasn't. (They'd made the mistake, they explained because I came from New York and talked with "a Jewish accent.") To be mistaken for a Jew was, in my mind, a compliment, not an insult. Since most of the kids who got into Hunter were Jewish, it's not surprising I concluded that Jews were smarter than other people.

My first brushes with anti-Semitism were baffling. It's been suggested to me that I'm as sensitive to anti-Semitism as Jews themselves. It may be that people who know that I'm not Jewish feel comfortable making anti-Semitic remarks in my presence, whereas they wouldn't say anything if someone Jewish were present. In some cases the anti-Semitism is so subtle or ingrained those expressing it deny it exists at all. A non-Jewish friend who used the word "Jew" to describe someone mercenary was surprised when I called her on it. "I'm not anti-Semitic," she protested, "why, some of my best friends are Jewish."

Some of my best friends are Jewish, too, but it's more than that. We goyim—Greeks and others—who've been embraced by the Jewish community in our youth have strong ties for life. Once a secret non-Jew in a Jewish world, I now see myself as a secret honorary Jew in a predominantly non-Jewish world. I think of how much we are shaped by the cultural identities we form in childhood. Every culture has its own set of priorities and preferences, humilities and arrogances, its own litany of assumptions. What I share with my Jewish friends is a similarity of upbringing. We come from homes where children were made much of, where intellectual activities were encouraged, where humor flourished right alongside of perennial anxiety about health, safety, and achievement. I also share with them a sense of vulnerability, the ghost of Anne Frank hovering in the dark corners of the future.

With Santa in the Oval, 1952

XVII

HOLIDAYS

Although the majority of residents were Jewish, Christmas was a holiday that Stuyvesant Town took seriously. Giant evergreen trees were set up in the fountain, tall as the spires of water in the summertime, a forest in the middle of the Oval. These trees were decorated with colored cardboard ornaments, disappointingly two-dimensional, but from my bedroom window at night they were a magnificent, illuminated jewel crown. Poorly concealed speakers beneath the branches piped out an endless circle of carols. Santa Claus made an annual stop at Stuyvesant Town, and on a cold outdoor throne listened to the requests of children, with their parents close beside. There was also a Santa at Macy's and another at Altman's, but I concluded they were mere apprentices to the genuine article who came to Stuyvesant Town.

Though I knew Christmas was a religious holiday, its religious aspects were barely noticed in my house. I had little wooden angels I'd bought in the basement of Woolworth's, but no crèche. We sang carols but never went near a church.

For my mother, I realize now, Christmas was an exhausting period of preparation, shopping, wrapping, and mailing. Each of my three uncles had produced four children, and my mother had to come up with presents for them all. Armed with a little notebook listing ages, and previous Christmas gifts, we'd go off to Macy's toy department. For an outlay of twelve gifts the yield was only three, and the fact that my cousins hadn't been raised to write thank-you notes, made my mother feel bitter towards my father. It wasn't so much his relatives' behavior as the fact that he refused to understand why she was bothered by it that made my mother angry. It was easy enough for my father to have a benevolent feeling about Christmas, since it was my mother—like most mothers I knew—who did all the work.

Getting the tree was one of my father's few duties. When I was little we walked to First Avenue, where trees transformed vacant lots into small forests. When I was older we went down to the piers along the Hudson River, where the trees were shipped into the city. The wind swept across the dark river, and men who worked under the eaves of the elevated West Side Highway huddled by a fire set in an old oil drum. The smell of that bonfire and the smell of the dark river, and the smell of the pine trees—immigrants from an alien world like Maine or Canada—all mingled. The trees were cheap, and inevitably a man would tell my father to "Just take one, for the kid," and my father would give the guy a bill anyway and wish him Merry Christmas. We'd stuff the tree in the trunk of the car, and my father would tie down the hood with some nylon parachute rope he acquired in The War. As we drove off I looked back and waved at the men, their faces orange by the firelight.

The tree we got was always too big for my mother and too small for me. It had to be tucked in the corner of the living room so it would not be visible from the door. My mother said that was because she did not want delivery boys to see it and expect holiday tips, but I think it had to do with her own ambivalence about Christmas itself.

Our tree was laden with ornaments, though I was not allowed tinsel (my mother considered it lower class) or spray-painted snow, which some of my friends carried to extremes on their mirrors and windows. The ugly ornaments went on the back of the tree, and my favorites competed for front center place. A few of each survive today. My favorite was one that was concave on one side, as if someone had punched it in and it had remained miraculously intact. Our lights were heavy things with thick wires that you couldn't disguise. Several of the bulbs had special candle attachments—liquid inside a glass vial that bubbled from the heat, at least they did on a few, rare occasions.

Christmas Eve we spent with my godparents' family, the only other Greeks we knew in Stuyvesant Town. They had a business that supplied the hot dog venders in the city, and so we traditionally had hot dogs there on Christmas Eve—along with fancier fare—and a big bag of them to take home with us. When we walked back to our apartment there always seemed to be snow just falling—but that's no doubt fantasy enhancing memory. It was the walking that was wonderful: the cold night, the trees lit up in the Oval, the carols in the air. How empty the place was!—all those windows and no one else outside. Stuyvesant Town seemed more like a sleepy, small town, a village even, than it ever seemed by day. That long walk home I would have had go on forever—for everything wonderful lay ahead. The night was thick with anticipation and promise. The great hush, the great peace that lay over Stuyvesant Town was part of the magic. I knew that somewhere Santa was frantic in preparation. It was like the breathless moment of dark silence in a theater, just before the curtain is lifted.

We had no fireplace so I hung my stocking on the door of the radio/phonograph cabinet. It was as close to the shape of a fireplace as any piece of furniture in our apartment could come, and appropriate, too, for it was where Tchaikovsky's Nutcracker Suite emanated from, produced by the four-record 78 rpm set. I and countless other little Stuyvesant Town girls had seen the *Nutcracker* at City Center, and we all longed to play Clara. In my nightgown I twirled around the freeform-shaped marble coffee table, between the two wings of the sectional sofa.

I had seen my mother wrapping presents late at night. I knew where she hid them—deep in the closet in her bedroom, beneath the mothball-laden garment bag that stored strapless dresses from her youth and my father's tuxedo. Yet I was as much a believer in Santa Claus as any child could be. In addition to the gifts from my parents there were always some presents Christmas morning whose origin was mysterious, not to mention the contents of my stocking. Santa came in through the window, I knew, and negotiated between floors on the pulley system the window washer used.

My mother's ambivalence towards Christmas was extreme. Though prudent about money, she bought me lavish toys—Madame Alexander dolls, Steiff stuffed animals, quantities of games and, of course, books. And long after I was too old to believe in Santa Claus, she carried on as his faithful surrogate. As gracious as she was about almost everything else, she hated receiving presents. All my gifts were supposed to be home-made. As a result my mother acquired numerous pincushions, aprons, and key chains, none of which she ever used. I had better success when I gave her original poetry, and once, at her request, a piano recital. My father's presents displeased my mother for years until he began putting his dental skills to work crafting her jewelry. This was jewelry my mother not only cherished but actually wore: silver seahorse earrings from melted down dimes and quarters (I knew it was a federal offense to melt down coins, but he risked it anyway), a microscope from melted-down gold inlays with a garnet for the focusing knob.

Christmas morning, half sleepless, I would run to the living room in the dark. It was always bleak outdoors. I would put on the tree lights, and in a state of near-drunk ecstasy examine the packages under the tree. Being an only child never seemed lonely then—it was a euphoric aloneness. I was allowed to open my stocking before my parents awoke, and I would take it back to bed with me. No matter how early I had gotten up, I was never able to fall back asleep. Once my parents were up and presents were opened, Christmas day got progressively depressing. Christmas night was the worst night of the year, for it was as far as could possibly be from the magic of Christmas Eve.

Unlike Christmas, Easter was a holiday we celebrated twice, as "regular" Easter and Greek Easter. Easter was an innocent, child-sweet holiday, in pastel tones. We dyed eggs in pale pinks and yellows and blues. The Easter bunny, whom I pictured as a Beatrix Potter rabbit infused with life, left a basket by my bed and a card saying how many eggs he had hidden in the living room. I didn't think he was capable of manipulating pulleys to gain entrance to Stuyvesant Town apartments, the way Santa did, so I concluded my parents must have run the extraordinary security risk of leaving our front door open a crack after they had gone to bed at night. Although we never went to church, I always wore my new spring coat, straw hat, and white gloves when we walked around Stuyvesant Oval.

Greek Easter was tied to Passover and depended on the mysterious migrations of the moon. It was a darker holiday—no bunnies or jellybeans. The eggs were all died a vicious red that stained your hands, the napkins and the white linen tablecloth. *Christos anesti!* ("Christ has risen") is what we wished everyone, and answered with *Alithos anesti!* ("Truly risen"). It was supposed to be a joyful declaration, but when I thought about what it meant I pictured the whole brutal saga, which involved nails and blood and agony, a story the Easter Bunny never invoked.

The lambs that I had imagined frolicking through flower-filled meadows at Easter were slaughtered for Greek Easter, and my grandmother made a special soup out of lambs' brains for our dinner, with my Uncle George's family. My four cousins—Carole, Marian, J.G. (George Jr.), and Alex—were all older, and made any holiday gathering exciting for me. As an only child I was fascinated by their sibling interactions. I fantasized that I was their youngest sister. No doubt they were more indulgent towards me than if I had been.

After dinner we had an egg-cracking party. My cousins and I had spent dinner time selecting our perfect egg. At first the eggs all looked alike, but as I studied them the distinctions magnified. Some eggs were squat, some were pointy, some had enamel-smooth shell, some had surfaces that were pimpled or gritty. Starting with the youngest (me) and oldest (my father's Uncle Alex) we tapped eggs against each other, point to point and tail to tail. There were various strategies and often (among my cousins) accusations of cheating. One egg was always smashed in the encounter, the other, remarkably, remained intact. The winner of the contest—it was never I—was the one left with an egg with one perfect end.

For Halloween we bought our pumpkin at D'Agostino's and carved it on the kitchen counter. We separated the seeds from the pulp, salted, and roasted them. The pulp was slimy, almost alive, saved from being something I wouldn't touch only by its fiercely orange color. We placed the pumpkin as a centerpiece in the dining area. The candle flame scarred the underside of the lid, filling our apartment with a smell, like burning leaves, I associated with fall in the country.

In Stuyvesant Town the fall leaves were not burnt. Armies of men gathered them up, the tines of their rakes pinging when they hit the edge of the paved paths. The grass, freshly uncovered, seemed unreal, a bright emerald green. The leaves were carted away and disposed of out of sight before a child could jump in any leaf pile.

The Five and Ten on First Avenue was filled with Halloween gear: masks and costumes and plastic spiders and cardboard skeletons whose jointed limbs could spin around 360 degrees. Some kids got to buy their costumes. They were a fabric close to paper and slipped on like a jumpsuit, with a little tie, that usually tore loose, at the neck. The front was imprinted—with skeleton bones or superman's insignia—the back was blank, as if you were two-dimensional. The masks smelled of rubber and made your face sweat and usually were carried by the string.

My mother pronounced the Five and Ten's offerings "cheesy," and made my costumes instead. One year I was a rabbit, one year I was a ghost. To keep the white sheet away from my face and give it some structure I wore an old fencing mask of my father's. He hadn't touched it for more than a decade, but it had been saved in the back of the closet, as if with extraordinary foresight. The mask smelled of rust, and wearing it was like looking through a screen door. One year I was a cat, a costume that had been made for a Halloween dancing school program. The ears and tail were real fur, salvaged from an old coat. I wore a black leotard and an orange crepe-paper tutu. This was a costume that my mother had saved. I found it in the back of her closet when I cleaned out the apartment, after she had died. It was in a garment bag with my mother's ancient Girl Scout uniform and my father's WWII officer's jacket, the tutu pressed against the khaki wool that had been through the Invasion. The crepe paper was no longer perky, but it had retained its orangeness, and my daughter wore the costume for Halloween.

One year I was a devil in red flannel pajamas, with a wire tail and a cape. My parents had brought me to a children's party held in the basement of the Greek Orthodox church in Brooklyn and were late picking me up. I ended up being the only child left, and the adult running the party had begun cleaning up. To keep myself busy I picked up a broom to sweep. Someone must have taken a picture of me, for it is there in the album, this devil going about God's work, cleaning a church basement. I look happy enough, but the picture lies, for I remember the terror I was feeling: I was certain that my parents hadn't turned up because they had been killed on the elevated highway that we took from Stuyvesant Town to Brooklyn, the road my father called a "death trap," and where I had seen the mangled bodies of cars. I stoically contemplated my future as an orphan, and wondered if I would be raised by my parents' friends Viola and Conrad, or my Uncle George and Aunt Bert. I put all my energy into my sweeping, and the helpful person waiting with me knew nothing at all of my anguish. How long did it last? It certainly wasn't many hours, as it felt; it was probably only an hour. When my parents arrived to pick me up, they were surprised to learn they had gotten the time wrong. I remember hearing, "Oh, it was no problem, she was such a good girl, worked so hard cleaning up." Only as we made our way out of the hall, did I throw myself, weeping, upon my bewildered mother.

"I thought you weren't coming," I cried. "I thought you were dead!" That's how little faith I had in God to protect my parents, to protect me, although he was presumably right there upstairs in that very church.

Weather was no impediment to trick-or-treating in Stuyvesant Town for I never had to go outside. I was able to ring a hundred doorbells in my building alone, twice that if I went through the carriage room to the adjoining building. Halloween was the only time when I was allowed in the stairways. I, and my band of friends, took the elevator up to Twelve and then made our way down, floor by floor. The stairways and hallways were crowded with costumed kids. The stairs were metal and clanged under our feet, and that airless stairwell echoed when some kid let loose a string of ghostly cries.

My friend Elaine lived in an apartment building uptown where there were no other children, and at Halloween her neighbors were usually unprepared with goodies and gave her money instead. In Stuyvesant Town you got candy or apples, and coins for your Unicef box. Some families kept their doors open all evening, a few had Halloween activities set up, like apple bobbing. When I had rung the last doorbell, down on T, I took the elevator back up to my apartment and dumped the contents of my shopping bag out on the coffee table. Then I helped my mother at the door, giving out our treats—diminutive boxes of raisins—a job that I later took over completely when I felt too old to trick-or-treat myself. I recognized many of the kids who came, and tried to guess who was behind the masks. Occasionally there would be children who didn't live in Stuyvesant Town, but came from the other side of First Avenue or Fourteenth Street. They always had the uneasy look of trespassers, as if they were afraid they would be found out and banished from these halls of privilege.

After eight it was older kids who rang the doorbell, packs of giggling teenagers with half-hearted costumes. Sometimes there would be a child alone, somewhat forlorn, like a guest left behind after the party is over. Before I got into bed I stood in my pajamas looking out the window. I could see the last groups of kids making their way from one building to another, and sometimes a lone ghost darting across the Oval, moving from one circle of streetlight to the next.

XVIII

CHINA

A curtain divided our Stuyvesant Town front hall closet into two territories. The front area, fit for the eyes of guests, was for coats only. In the depths behind, hidden from view, my mother stowed away the shopping cart, the carpet sweeper, the shoe-shine box, suitcases, a cardboard box filled with old wedding presents she'd never used, a box of souvenirs of World War II. At the very back of the closet was a box that held relics from Uncle Alex's wholesale store—glasses and planters and figurines—some acquired when Uncle Alex was alive, some leftovers from the business when he died. Periodically my mother would be inspired to forage in this collection, and the entire closet would be emptied so the box could be dragged out. She would plead with me not to unpack everything, but it was impossible to free only one item from its tissue paper cocoon, without wanting to see them all. Invariably my mother would decide that although she couldn't bring herself to get rid of any of it, there was nothing that she wanted to bring out into the light of her home.

"Someday I'll give all of this away," she said, but the box was still there when I had to empty the closet after she died.

Great Uncle Alexander Vlachos, my grandmother's brother, was married to a woman of Scandinavian descent, Aunt Minnie, but for the last twenty years they barely spoke. He was an imposing figure, with the eyes of a snake charmer, eyebrows thick as a moustache, and tufts of hair sprouting from his ears. My grandmother was a widow for most of my life, and it was Uncle Alex who took her out for Sunday drives in his black DeSoto with the running boards, sometimes driving way below the speed limit, with a pack of honking cars in his wake, sometimes so fast that once the passenger door flew open and my grandmother was saved only because her coat had gotten caught on the armrest. Uncle Alex sat next to my grandmother at family holiday dinners. Aunt Minnie, for reasons mysterious to me, never appeared. I accepted this as a child, as children accept all the strange relationships among the adults they grow up with. The only time Aunt Minnie was ever in our Stuyvesant Town apartment was right after Uncle Alex died, when I was around ten. I remember her sitting on the piano bench, her shoulders hunched over, her pale blond hair falling across her face.

"Oh, he was such a good man, such a good man!" she said over and over again.

Uncle Alex had a wholesale flower supply business in the heart of the flower district, a short bus ride from Stuyvesant Town, on West Twenty-eighth Street. The flower district was close to the fur district, both industries dominated by Greek entrepreneurs. My father's dental office was located close by.

Uncle Alex's shop was a narrow building, four stories high. The street was lined with businesses that sold wholesale plants and flowers—living things. Uncle Alex dealt in the lifeless: china, glass, metal, clay. He had lead crystal vases from Czechoslovakia, hammered brass planters from Greece, ceramic candy dishes from Italy, porcelain from China, and a vast array of china figurines from Japan.

"Junk," my mother said.

In the front window of the store was a Chinese vase, taller than my father, covered with figures and designs outlined in gold.

"Now that," said my mother, "might be worth a small fortune."

The store had narrow aisles that ran the depth of the building, lined with wooden shelves from floor to ceiling, packed with merchandise. There were dozens of each item, usually identical, some still swaddled in grey tissue paper, some with packing straw or bits of grey tissue paper still clinging to their shiny surface. The shelves were so deep I can't imagine how anyone reached in to the back when the front guard had been sold, or how the shelves were ever restocked. There were a few lightbulbs dangling from strings, but Uncle Alex was as parsimonious with electricity as he was with most everything else. The place was accustomed to getting by on whatever natural light managed to penetrate the windows, which surely in my father's lifetime had never been washed. There was less dust than you would have expected—perhaps because the windows were never opened— and the store had an almost pleasant smell, part hayloft, part Museum of Natural History. The building was unheated, except for a small space heater reluctantly called to duty on the coldest days, near Uncle Alex's desk in the front. It was the antithesis of our sunny, over-heated Stuyvesant Town: the chill, the dimness, the clutter.

How Uncle Alex kept track of his inventory I'll never know. Even in the gloom he managed to find anything he wanted, though there were no labels on the shelves. Price lists and ordering information were stored somewhere in his head. My grandfather Guizot (my mother's father and not related to Uncle Alex) was his accountant. He slaved over the store's books and tried to make sense of whatever written records he could find. Scrupulously honest, my grandfather was constantly in despair over Uncle Alex's casual attitude towards the Internal Revenue Service.

"They'll lock you up!" my grandfather wailed.

"What, a poor old man like me?" Uncle Alex laughed.

"They'll come here and investigate the business!" my grandfather said.

"So they come here. What will they see?" asked Uncle Alex.

And what would they see? Uncle Alex, in a poorly patched grey cardigan, in his unlit, unheated warehouse, eating his lunch at his desk: his lunch the meager cheese sandwich that Aunt Minnie delivered, wordlessly, every day.

When we visited Uncle Alex's store, he would serve my parents Greek coffee, brewed in a copper pot on his single burner stove, and encourage me to go off exploring on my own. My mother was nervous about my wandering alone in what she called that "firetrap of a building," but she was cornered into acquiescence by her code of politeness (which she applied in all dealings with my father's relatives) combined with my father's perverse refusal to share her evaluation of the dangers. In addition to her anxiety about my safety, my mother also suffered because of Uncle Alex's urging me to help myself to whatever I wanted. I'm not sure if this was because she feared his more hideous chachkas would desecrate our apartment, or if it was merely her deep-seated qualms about being beholden in any way to anyone in my father's family.

I was as afraid of that ancient building as I was drawn by its secrets. I would make my way cautiously up the narrow wooden stairs and up and down the aisles, wary of treacherous floor boards and rats (though it was unlikely a rat would choose to inhabit such a cold place, where there was no edible morsel), scouting for treasures. The eyes of ceramic cats and china figurines followed me in the semidarkness. Sometimes I'd be startled by a rustling sound or a speck of light glinting off a glazed surface.

There were infinite shelves of dull vases and pots, but I always found china certainly designed for a child: a donkey with baskets to hold a cactus plant, a cookie jar in the shape of a hippo, a Santa with a ceramic beard and fur that looked soft but was prickly to touch.

"Take two!" Uncle Alex urged me, first in English, then in Greek. "Take a dozen."

I saved for last the metal unit of little drawers, which stood near the front of the shop. Each drawer was filled with miniatures, most designed for bonsai or terrariums. There were thumb-sized wooden Chinese men pulling rickshaws. There were painted lead bridges and park benches scaled for lightning bugs. There were plastic Scotty dogs and gilt kittens and tiny dioramas with mirrors in the back. Best of all were the blown-glass swans, which were supposed to work as barometers (when you filled them with colored water through a pinhole in the neck) but never did. The paper instructions that accompanied each one stated: "We do not guarantee this to be accurate but it is something the whole family will enjoy as well as being a very colorful decoration for the home. This is styled merchandise and the last word in good taste." We used them for Christmas tree ornaments, hanging them up with fishing line tied around their throats.

My mother allowed Uncle Alex to press upon her boxes of my favorites. She was forced to admit that they made excellent favors for my birthday parties.

Uncle Alex had no children, and my father was his favorite nephew. When my father was a boy Uncle Alex had a retail florist business, and my father worked for him after school delivering flowers. He recruited all his neighborhood friends to work for Uncle Alex during the Christmas and Easter rush.

In my warm, pink bedroom in Stuyvesant Town, surrounded by my arsenal of stuffed animals, I ask my father to tell me a goodnight story about when he was a little boy, the story of Uncle Alex's wager.

It was Christmas time and the weather was wicked. Uncle Alex had an order for a plant to be delivered to Staten Island.

"You'll never get a boy to deliver that for you," said a friend who had stopped by the store, and he and Uncle Alex ended up betting money on it.

It looked as if Uncle Alex would lose the bet, as one by one the boys refused to make the trip. My father was not only the youngest boy who worked for Uncle Alex, but he was small for his age. Uncle Alex asked him last. My father took the plant, without question. Uncle Alex gave him change for the subway and the ferry to Staten Island, and wrote directions for him on a slip of paper, and my father set off. He'd never been to Staten Island before in his life.

With each telling of the story, the plant gets heavier, my father gets smaller, the wind blows colder, the crossing to Staten Island gets rougher, and Staten Island itself gets farther away. But in every version my father returns safely, with a half dollar tip in his pocket ("a fortune in those days"), and Uncle Alex wins his bet.

As a child I thought of my father's bravery. Now I think of his sweet, blind obedience and the cruelty of a man sending a little boy off on such a mission. My father remembers him for his generosity, remembers that Uncle Alex helped him out with money for his college tuition.

When Uncle Alex died, everything in the store was liquidated. The huge vase in the front window was discovered to have a crack in it and its value was negligible. Uncle Alex left everything he had to his wife, Aunt Minnie, and nothing to his sister, my grandmother, who carried on at his funeral as if she were the real widow.

When Aunt Minnie died she left my father enough money for him to remodel his dental office, but the bulk of what turned out to be a considerable estate, went to the Bide-A-Wee Bird Home, though she and Uncle Alex never had a bird or any other pet.

The three Demas brothers in 1932—my father
on the shoulders of John (left) and George

XIX

SUBWAYS

Whenever we drove past the Port Authority Bus terminal, my father would point out the window and say, "That's where I was born." He had been born, in 1909, in a tenement that had been torn down to make space for the terminal, and it was not buses, but subway trains that were the cadence of my father's early years. His building was on Ninth Avenue, between Forty-first and Forty-second Streets, his apartment level with the tracks of the Ninth Avenue elevated subway, the "El," so the trains roared by his window. The neighborhood was not that far from Stuyvesant Town, and it was considered so tough it was called Hell's Kitchen, the name a strange juxtaposition of the domestic and the damned.

My father's grandmother, Marigo (that "g" in Greek pronounced as softly as a mere clearing of the throat), a midwife, had delivered him, as she had most of the Greek-American children of my father's generation who lived in that part of the city. Her photographs show a handsome, strong-jawed woman with thick braids wound on her head. Her husband had emigrated from Sparta to New York ahead of her, but when she arrived with their three children she found he had been less faithful to her than she to him, so she found her own place, earned her own living, and raised the children on her own. She was a single, working mother, a century before the role acquired its title. My father remembers when this errant grandfather visited them, when he was a boy, his grandmother refused to come out of the kitchen to see him.

"What do I need him for now?" she asked.

It sounds even more emphatic in the original Greek, which was, I now learned, the only language she spoke, in spite of the fact that she lived in New York at least half her life. In her little community, Greek was the only language she needed. Her daughter, Alexandra, my grandmother, was bilingual, but could read and write well only in Greek. My father, the next generation, spoke Greek at home, but had to go to afterschool classes to learn to read and write Greek. True to the typical pattern of immigrant assimilation, my knowledge of Greek was sketchy at best, a faint echo from the past.

When my father was five his parents moved up in the world, literally uptown to a third-floor railroad flat on West Sixty-sixth Street, across the street from the High School of Commerce, which he later attended. His grandmother, who'd lived with them for years, eventually got her own apartment a few blocks west. My father went to P.S. 87, an eleven-block walk. He got a nickel for lunch and he would team up with another kid who had a nickel. One bought a loaf of bread, the other the baloney. They'd slice the bread up the middle and make a hero sandwich to share. After school my father and his two brothers trekked across Central Park to Greek School, at the Greek Orthodox Cathedral on East Seventy-second Street. On cold days he was given a hot potato, to warm his hands while he walked and eat when he got there.

There was no hint of former beauty in my grandmother's jowly face, nor was there beauty in the face in photographs of her when she was young. She thought well of her looks, though—you can see that in her pose. She was strict with her three sons and my father remembers little affection from her. This maternal lapse was compensated for by the affection from his grandmother and his genial father, Constantine (my mother's father's name was also Constantine), who had a well-fed look appropriate to his business, which was supplying meat wholesale to the Greek restaurants.

In one of my favorite stories my father would tell me about when he was a little boy, he and his brothers, John and George, had gotten into trouble, and had been sent to their bedroom to wait for their father to mete out punishment when he returned from work. When their father came home, their mother recounted their crime, and though he argued in favor of leniency, she demanded he be tough. So finally, his father took off his belt and went to the bedroom to deal with the boys. My father and his brothers had been waiting in fear, but once the bedroom door was shut their father winked at them. He instructed them to run back and forth across the room screaming, which they did with considerable zeal, while he whipped his belt against the bedpost. This arrangement proved of great satisfaction to everyone involved.

When my father was a teenager his parents made their last move, to a row house in the Bensonhurst section of Brooklyn, the first piece of American soil the family owned. It was a two-story brick house, three windows wide. When they first lived there Sixty-fourth Street was unpaved, and my grandfather's car one of the few on the block.

My grandmother was widowed when I was a baby, and she converted the upstairs of her house to an apartment, which she rented out. The former dining room became her bedroom. On her dresser top was a cluster of icons illuminated by a red light, the kind of religious display that seemed perpetually mysterious, and filled me with unease. It was a dark, sober bedroom that seemed already to have the character of its final duty, for it was the room my grandmother died in. She was late in her eighties at the time and died, as my father joked, of nothing serious. Indeed, she had been feeling well up to her last day, and though she had summoned a priest to her bedside no one expected the dénouement.

At the front of the house, in a patch of dirt the area of my desk top, my grandmother grew roses. They bloomed profusely, fertilized with kitchen scraps, a shade of red that clashed with the color of the brick. An enclosed sunporch overlooked the street, and my grandmother crocheted at her post there, while she kept her eye on the doings of the neighborhood. The open shelves that divided the sunroom from livingroom were lined with photographs of my uncles and my father and my cousins and me in two-sided frames. Some of us looked out towards my grandmother and the street, and others looked back to the dark interior of the house. My father and his brothers were each captured in uniform, one for each branch of the military: Uncle John, the Army Air Force, Uncle George, the Navy, and my father, who always preferred the hard ground to air or sea, the regular Army. (All three had returned from World War II unscathed.)

Behind the back of the house, outside the kitchen, were a porch and a yard. Just beyond the concrete wall at the back was the most remarkable feature of my grandmother's house: the Sea Beach line BMT subway. In this part of Brooklyn it was subway level, but open air, like railroad tracks. Every fifteen minutes or so the express train would come roaring past, shaking the bones of the house, rattling everything in it. The more frequent local screeched to a halt at the station half a block away. When you sat out on the porch you'd look across a wide chasm to the back yards of the houses on the next street over. If you kept your eyes level you could have a rural fantasy and imagine that all that lay between you and those other backyards was a field or a river. The porch was covered by a grape arbor. Though the grapes hung purple and tantalizing from the vines, they were the wrong kind, as I rediscovered every time I tried to eat one. My grandmother picked the tender, young grape leaves for *yaprikia,* stuffed grape leaves. The grapes she picked for her neighbors, the Levines, who made them into what she called "Jewish" wine. The train was too low for passengers to see up at an angle to the porch. It was a pity, for they could have shared in those rural fantasies when they caught a glimpse of an old woman with a basket on her arm, picking grapes from her arbor.

My father, who was sensitive to the noises of our Stuyvesant Town neighbors, and banged on the ceiling with a broom handle when the woman upstairs walked across the floor in high heels after he had gone to bed, claims not have been disturbed by the sound of the subway behind the house all the years he lived there. Perhaps it was because he had been reared in the din of the Ninth Avenue El.

Perhaps it was because trains had a different meaning then. For my father growing up they were the sound of progress, speed, efficiency. They were the modern world, visible right from the back doorstep.

Though the humans adapted to this strange neighbor, the biorhythms of their pets may have been disturbed. My grandmother's bull terrier was a nervous dog with bulging eyes who ran a circular path through kitchen, bedroom, living room. He'd jump in the air for an apple and choke it down, core and all. His predecessor reportedly had committed suicide by leaping from the concrete wall down into the path of an oncoming train.

When a train passed by, the basement trembled. I imagined it right there, separated from us by only a bank of dirt. I wondered if the ground might cave in and we would find ourselves facing windows of startled commuters.

The basement was a long narrow room, with a round oak table in the middle. At the street side of the house was the vestigial coal bin. The whitewashed cement walls were always cool to the touch, even when it was hot upstairs, and were hung with pictures of ancestors that for some reason had not been quite worthy of being displayed upstairs. The living room had parlor status, off-limits for most of the time, so it was in the basement that my father spent so many hours of his youth. It was at this round table that his father sat with him and his brothers to map out their futures. He laid out the possible occupations available, and then divided them up, according to what they seemed best suited for and what was best for the family. John, the oldest, would go to school to be an accountant, my father, the middle one, would go to dental school, and the youngest, George would go to law school. Each son dutifully followed the path that had been decided upon. A generation later, when we joined my Uncle George's family at my grandmother's house for a holiday dinner, since there was no dining room, the meal was served on this table in the basement.

When my father and I periodically visited my grandmother for dinner on a weekday night, my mother stayed home. We'd leave her at her desk, sitting on her stool, grading biology lab reports. It was understood that she didn't join us because during the week she had too much work, but it was certainly true that my mother had no interest in visiting my grandmother, and my grandmother never was sorry that my mother didn't come.

My cousin J.G. often joined us for dinner, and since there were just four of us, we ate in the kitchen, which was convenient, for my grandmother spent the entire meal on her feet, refilling our plates. She seemed happy, then, a woman who was not naturally inclined to such a state. She'd even laugh at the endless riddles and knock-knock jokes my cousin provided for these occasions. I'd try to remember the best of them to take back to my friends, though they never sounded as funny outside of my grandmother's kitchen.

It was usually dark when my father and I drove back to Stuyvesant Town, the lights twinkling along the Brooklyn Bridge and the Manhattan Bridge beside it, as we crossed over to Manhattan. The East River, black and bottomless, was the river that separated my father's past, and my grandmother's old-fashioned ways, from us. Stuyvesant Town, in contrast to the house in Brooklyn, seemed sleek and modern and ascetic. It was like returning to the contemporary world.

Back in the apartment we'd find my mother sitting over her desk. She'd eaten dinner on her own, cleaned up the kitchen, and laid out breakfast for the morning, but she was just as we had left her, the stack of lab reports several inches higher on the right than on the left.

When my father was given money for college tuition by his Uncle Alex, he and his mother went to pick it up in person. It was two hundred dollars, cash, and his Aunt Minnie had folded the bills twice and tied them up in a handkerchief. She tied one end of a string around the neck of the bundle, the other end to the belt loop of his pants. The little wad of money was lowered into his pocket, and his hand held it there. He was fifteen years old and embarrassed by the string, by the fact that his mother had insisted on coming with him, but he was also terrified. He and his mother walked to the subway, pressed together, like fettered convicts. On the train ride home they wedged close, the pocket, the wad of money, his hand, squashed between them. His left hand clutched the pole as the train headed out from the station, but soon was slippery with sweat. He wiped it off on his pants, then buried it between his legs. Handless, he watched everyone watching him. It was not that many blocks, but it felt like the longest train ride he had ever taken in his life, and the names of the stations planted themselves in his memory, like facts.

When my father was little, he told me, he had believed that subways burrowed their own tunnels. And that was the only comfort to him then, on that long subway ride, his childhood fantasy of the train as a splendid worm, digging its way under Manhattan and under the river and out into the open trenches through the country, Bensonhurst and Bay Ridge. I loved that image, the idea of the subways as underground creatures, digging their way through the substrata of Manhattan and Brooklyn.

For me, the tiled subway stations were like small planets lit up in the solar system, and the train was a shuttle, hurtling through black space. Sometimes, for no reason, the train would come to an abrupt halt in the middle of a tunnel and the lights would all go out. There was no greater darkness anywhere in the world.

When I entered seventh grade, Hunter High School, I took the IRT subway to school instead of the Lexington Avenue bus. The subway was a smoother ride and I was able to read and do my homework. The cross-town bus drivers became familiar (some perennially cheerful, some constitutionally grumpy), but I rarely saw the motorman on the subway. The trains seemed to drive themselves.

I had a student pass for both bus and subway. Inevitably when I was late for school the token seller would be occupied with customers and I would be waving my pass while a train prepared to leave the station. If the gate buzzed open in time, I'd run for it, sometimes wedging my tote bag into the narrowing train doorway. Theoretically the train was not able to take off if the doors weren't closed, but I'd yank back my bag if the doors didn't immediately part for me to enter. When I just missed a train the desolation on the platform seemed impenetrable. The train took with it all the light, all the noise, and left behind eddies of dust and gum wrappers.

I was not always afraid on the subways, but I was always on guard. Once standing up at a pole in a crowded train I felt someone's hand in my pocket. I studied the faces of the people close to me, and there was no clue about whose hand it might be. I considered snatching the hand and holding it up to be claimed, instead I slapped it hard as I could and it was withdrawn quickly.

Once, while I was reading, an older friend sitting next to me whispered, "Don't look up." I did, of course. There was something hanging out from the open trench coat of the man holding on to the strap above me. At first I wasn't sure what it was—it looked like a slimy sea creature, a squid, perhaps. Then I realized it was the man's penis, but it seemed to be something wrong with it, for it was oozing some substance. I lowered my head quickly. When our stop came my friend grabbed my hand and I pushed past without looking, and ran off the train, down the station, stumbling up the stairs to the air above. I ran into the office of the principal, crying. My friend must have explained what happened, because I was unable to. I did not know why I was so frightened, but I couldn't stop crying and I got excused from my morning classes.

I was forever wary of men in trench coats. I was wary of men in general, and if they stood over me when I had a seat on the subway I did not look up. Once, when the train stopped at the Forty-second Street station, a man standing by the door caught my eye and grinned. Then he opened his coat to reveal his penis—this one small as a thumb. The local train, which I rode, was waiting at the stop for the express, which came roaring in on the neighboring platform. When the doors started closing the man stepped back onto the platform. I had a quick image of his penis caught in the door—proof of his exposure—but he pulled back just in time and the train took off. He was an ordinary man, well dressed, well kempt, going off to a job somewhere. Perhaps he was someone's husband. Perhaps he was someone's father. He did not look any different from the Stuyvesant Town daddies I knew. Except for the way he looked at me—a knowing, mean little grin—and the fact that beneath his double-breasted trench coat his fly was unzipped.

Most often I took only the Lexington Avenue line, and then changed for the cross-town bus. On some occasions though, I took the subway down to Fourteenth Street and transferred to the Canarsie Line, which ran east. The Fourteenth Street, Herald Square station was an underground city, and it was a hike between connecting trains. I stayed on the main path, avoided dark tunnels, dead ends. There was a bazaar of stalls, a marketplace that never saw the light. This whole emporium was an underworld of cheap things: two dollar umbrellas, seventy-five cent bunches of flowers, stones polished bright as gems, for only a dollar. It was a child's world of junk, and it smelled like the circus—cotton candy and popcorn. On occasion I bought a pretzel—something my mother would never have allowed—and ate it furtively, expecting any moment to get violently ill from all the germs in the open stand. The Canarsie Line had older trains on it than the Lexington Avenue Line—rattan seats and ceiling fans like old propeller planes. It seemed almost foreign, and there was indeed the fear that if I missed my stop, First Avenue, I would be swept east, right under the East River itself, to that far country: Brooklyn.

When I came up from the subway at First Avenue, it was like emerging from Hades itself. On the south side of the street lay lower Manhattan, tenements with fire escapes, on the north side was Stuyvesant Town, its great brick wall of buildings holding back that teeming part of the city. Compared to the blocks south of Fourteenth Street, Stuyvesant Town was a peaceful garden, the pace of a different life.

Our new Mercury, 1959

XX
CARS

For nine years of my childhood my parents drove a 1950 Mercury, whom we called "Merc." I was three when we bought it. How strange it seemed to see cars indoors in the showroom, placed around like furniture. I climbed into the back seat of one model and peeked into the ashtray built into the armrest, like a miniature treasure chest with a lid that snapped shut. I curled up on the seat and went to sleep. Later I learned that was what sold my father on the car. It was a two-door coupe and he felt the back seat was safe for a child.

Merc was dark green and had itchy brown wool seat covers. My parents previous car had been a navy blue Nash Rambler, and the blue had turned a mottled purple, like an oil slick on water. My mother would never buy a blue car after that. Even twenty years later she was convinced that auto manufacturers couldn't make a blue that didn't fade.

Although the back seat was perfect for kids, I usually rode in the front, next to the window, with my mother in the middle and my father at the wheel. My mother drove on her own, but never when my father was in the car. There were no seatbelts then, and whenever we were in a situation my mother deemed dangerous (she was a nervous passenger and always anticipating peril) her arm shot across in front of me and she grabbed the window handle. I've read in some reliable source that in a crash people can't hold on like that and such a technique would be quite useless, but my mother's protective love was so fierce I am certain she would have proven the exception to that rule.

I was too young to enjoy Merc as a new car. It seemed to be an old car for most of my childhood, a car that I was increasingly embarrassed of and mortified by. Cars, I believed, revealed to the outside world your status and your wealth. My parents' car was fully paid for (my mother would never buy anything "on time"), but there was no solace for me in that; I envied friends who had new cars, even if they were financed by loans. What I knew was the agony of waiting to be picked up outside our apartment building (my mother and I often waited by the curb near our front door while my father fetched the car) and having kids I knew witness me getting into the old, outdated, dirty vehicle. My parents didn't share my shame. In fact they didn't understand it at all.

When my father had first come home from The War, my parents had driven a Cadillac. My mother joked about that car—they'd gotten it used, it was "repainted" (and in her mind, therefore, not to be trusted) and unreliable. I seized on the name Cadillac, the very fact of it, and liked to let my friends know that it had been part of my heritage. I referred to it as a "Caddy," my parents' term and was impressed by my own cheekiness.

When my Uncle George got rich he bought a black Cadillac, and on one blessed occasion he picked us up in front of our apartment house. I looked around as I stepped in, hoping kids I knew would see my grand exit, and then, as we drove out of Stuyvesant Town, kept my face close to the window so I could be seen. To be seen in such a car! When my grandmother died I got to ride in a limousine from the church in Brooklyn to the cemetery in Queens. I felt like the daughter of a diplomat, and kept watching from the car window for children in passing cars who would see and envy me. No matter that we were following a hearse.

As for my family's old Merc, she did not age gracefully. When "fins" came into style in the late fifties, the Mercury's smooth curves looked as old-fashioned as my grandfather's ancient Oldsmobile. Janie, a Hunter classmate, was the first kid whose family got a car with fins and it seemed to fly around Stuyvesant Town Oval. For quite a while Janie, an otherwise unnoticed child, was the center of attention in school.

One night some car racing down the exit ramp of East River Drive took a spin and landed on Merc, parked below. The passenger side door was crunched in, but the car still ran perfectly and my father wasn't ready to give it up. My father fastened a rope to the inside of the door and when he went around corners my mother hung on to the rope and kept the door from swinging out. I rode in the back seat.

Finally, in 1959, my parents decided to buy a new car, another Mercury. We got a white one, against all my mother's protests and our better sense, for how could you possibly keep a car white when you parked under the Viaduct? The dealer offered my father only $25 for Merc, and my father was so angry he stalked out of the showroom and we almost didn't get a new car at all. In the end he had to pay a junker $10 to take it away, but he seemed to mind that less than the initial insult.

My mother liked the new car because the front seat went up and down automatically, and for once she could see out the front properly while she drove, though she drove rarely and was always nervous when she did. Her fear of driving was confirmed the one time she and I were alone on East River Drive. Suddenly we were driving into a blank wall—although the car didn't stop and there was no sense of impact. My mother screamed and braked. It was the great white hood of the car, which had come unlatched and sprung up in our faces. Miraculously we were not rear-ended. Miraculously my mother got out of the car and slammed the hood down tight without getting run over. Most miraculously of all, she managed to summon the courage to drive us home.

The White Car (as we called it) was so beautiful to me that for months after I still could not truly believe it was ours. It was not so much the pleasure of being seen in such a car, it was the pleasure of being in it all on its own. And strangely, even when it aged and was no longer in fashion, I got a whiff of remembered euphoria every time I rode in it. The car was so spacious that I could sit on the floor in the front seat. The interior was "gold"—gold carpeting (little loops of thread that perked back upright the first few times after you stepped on them and forever after that lay flat), gold leatherette seats, which were immediately encased in clear vinyl seatcovers, and a spongy gold leatherette dashboard to cushion your head in case of an accident.

This was the car I learned to drive in. It was too wide to fit into the garage of our house in Mt. Kisco. It was impossible to parallel-park in any parking space. The power steering had a dreamlike quality. It was like driving a ballroom.

Our next car, a Chrysler Imperial, was a hand-me-down from my Uncle George. My mother, who was penurious but despised charity, fought long with my father over accepting it. But my father was delighted to accept any bounty of his younger brother's corporate success, and besides he liked the car. It was dark green with a leatherette roof, and it, too, did not fit inside our garage in Mt. Kisco. The front seats were two huge, black leather armchairs, which reclined. The dashboard was paneled with real wood. The leather armrests opened to reveal plastic lined compartments where you could, I imagined, keep ice for your champagne. At home we had a radio with a single speaker. This car had a stereo system. My father and I would enjoy just sitting in the car, not going anyplace, switching the four speakers and playing with the treble and the bass.

Once my father backed the Chrysler into a wall and crunched off a piece of the body around the wheel. He assiduously tamped the surviving metal back into shape, and then created a giant inlay behind it (he was dentist after all) out of some mixture of plaster and putty, to reinforce it. He painted it dark green to match the car.

Another time, when my parents were driving past a demolition site on Twenty-third Street, a piece of rubble the size of a basketball fell off a building and landed on the car. Had it gone through the windshield it would surely have killed them. Instead it landed on the hood. It did not damage the engine, either, and my father was able to bang the hood back into shape. The rubble turned out to be a piece of stone cornice from the roof trim of the building, and my mother saved it as an ornament for our garden in Mt. Kisco, this piece of a frieze, once visible only to New York pigeons, brought down to earth.

XXI

KISCO

Just around the time I was born, my Guizot grandparents bought property in Mt. Kisco, a town an hour north of New York City, and began to build a house. The construction of the house paralleled my own most amazing changes. I was an infant looking up at the undersides of leaves from my bassinet while they studied blueprints on the grass beside me. When I was old enough to sit up, the foundation was dug. When I was old enough to stand, the house was framed in, and I practiced walking along planks lying on the ground. The house was finished when I was old enough to do a somersault on the living room floor.

My grandparents had worked all their lives, saving money to build this house, and they paid for it in installments as the construction progressed, right up to the $9,000 total. They would no more have considered a mortgage than robbing a bank.

The house was built to withstand snowstorms, hurricanes, earthquakes, and whatever tribulations nature might deal out. The bottom half of it was stone in the front and brick on the sides, the upper half was white clapboard. It reminded me of a girl with a white shirt on top and a wool plaid skirt below—the costume I wore to school. The house was set close to the road because my grandfather didn't want to have to shovel a long driveway. At that time the road was narrow and rarely traveled. Years later when the road got busier, they regretted that the house hadn't been set back on the property, but that brick and stone fortress was as immovable as our building in Stuyvesant Town.

Behind the house there was an avenue of maples, an old section of road the new one had replaced. Up on the hill was a well-buried foundation of an old house, and a flat area by the old road where a barn had been. Only jewelweed grew there. Higher up on the mountain, I discovered a circular concrete pool filled in with clay, a cistern where a spring still bubbled mysteriously from the rock. An octogenarian neighbor, who lived in his ancestral farmhouse, told us how travelers would stop along the road and go up to that spring for water. At that time there was a deep well. Once, he said, a carriage stopped there, and a man and woman were arguing. Only the man drove on. This was a tale my mother would have censored, but it was too late. I kept wondering if the woman's body was still there at the bottom, buried under the silt and earth.

Children love archaeological adventures—unearthing artifacts, uncovering stories. In Stuyvesant Town digging was not allowed, and our clandestine excavations never turned up anything we hadn't buried ourselves. There were no relics of the past in Stuyvesant Town. All traces of the lives that had been lived in that part of Manhattan had been scrubbed from the soil. It was as if the buildings had risen out of virgin fields, as if the territory had never been inhabited before.

On the hillside in Mt. Kisco, in a pile of rubble, I found a clay pipe dating from the eighteenth century. In the woods I found the metal rim from an old carriage wheel. The place trembled with history, all there underground. We were living right on top of its secrets. If I were an adult then, I would have gone to town records, found out what I could about the property's past, but my grandparents didn't have that sense of curiosity—they were fixed on the future. The rubble of ordinary people two hundred years before held no magic for them; they had both grown up in Greece and were schooled in truly ancient ruins.

For my grandfather, who had spent the main part of his life living in rented apartments—in the Bronx, in upper Manhattan, in Queens—owning property in Mt. Kisco was a fantasy made real. The place lived up to his dream and he was as blind to its flaws as Chekhov's character in "Gooseberries" is blind to the imperfections of his country estate.

The four acres of Westchester county land were lush. My grandfather bought a book called *Four Acres and Independence* and proceeded to create a life for himself. He was a weekend farmer—commuting to the city during the week. Up on the hillside in a clearing, he planted a small orchard, two of each: apple, pear, peach, and cherry, and a single quince tree. Farther up the hillside, without benefit of power tools, he cleared woods for a garden. As the first settlers on that same land had, he felled trees, pulled up roots, and planted vegetables. It was too far from the house for a hose, so my grandfather hand-carried buckets of water up there every day. The surrounding forest allowed the garden minimal sun, but the soil was rich. Pumpkin vines escaped out of the garden into the forest and climbed the trees, and in September pumpkins hung from the maples and black walnut.

In the back yard my grandfather built a coop for chickens and ducks. The chickens had nesting boxes with little doors that allowed access from the outside. No one had heard of cholesterol then, so my grandfather's health regime included a raw egg a day—during the chickens' brief productive period—and on occasion I joined him. One by one the fowl were decimated by a weasel, who got into the coop by mysterious means and performed his bloody deed by night. The last duck, named Coryanna, survived a weasel attack and was elevated to household pet.

My grandmother developed breast cancer, had a mastectomy, and died anyway, in that house, around the time I was five. She was cremated. Her ashes resided in a polished wooden box, the size of a doll's trunk, on the dresser, with a photograph of her propped against it, and then were buried under a dogwood tree in the front yard. I called it Yiya's tree (*Yiya* is Greek for grandmother) and believed that it was her ashes that sent forth those blossoms. I buried my face in them, and they seemed like skin, her embrace.

My grandfather went around for months in a fit of grief. He stayed with us in Stuyvesant Town, carrying on, having my mother wait on him, helpless. Then he took a trip to Greece and returned miraculously remarried. He brought his new wife, Athena, back to Mt. Kisco with him. She had married what she thought was a rich American who owned a beautiful country estate. She found herself in a two-bedroom prison, married to a man who wept about his first wife, went off to work in the city while she was left to face cold winters she had never known before, snow she had never imagined before, in a town where she knew no one, unable to drive, unable to speak English, and resistant to learning.

I take her part now, but only in that paragraph. I hated her. She did her best to bribe me—chocolates, dolls, jewelry—but I wasn't game. When she pulled me on her lap she squeezed so tight her bracelets pressed into my skin. Her kisses—which crescendoed in my grandfather's presence—left red lipstick marks on my cheeks and neck. My mother forced me to be polite, but she and I were allies against this interloper.

My grandfather's wife had lied about her age to my grandfather when she married him, but suddenly admitted to an extra decade when she found out about social security benefits. She had never been married before, had no children, but she had an extensive collection of nieces and nephews whom she expected my grandfather to favor with a steady stream of gifts and money. She badgered him constantly about moving back to Greece and finally wore him down till he acquiesced. I now had a rational reason for hating her: she was stealing my grandfather away with her to a foreign land.

My mother bought the house in Mt. Kisco from her father and with that money he bought a house in Athens, where his wife ruled, and my grandfather, trapped and miserable, wrote us weekly letters detailing the idiocy of her relatives.

And so began their many years of embattled marriage. My grandfather inflicted small cruelties on his wife—refusing to eat the cake she baked for him, criticizing her attire, insulting her opinions—in order to assuage the ghost of my grandmother. And my grandfather's wife, false stoic, pseudo martyr, lamented constantly, and wielded her power. She involved him in schemes in Greece and forced him to change his will so her relatives, not his children, would inherit whatever he had. My grandfather dragged her back to the United States periodically for extended visits, and took up residence in the house in Mt. Kisco.

My grandfather and I loved to go for hikes in the woods. He was so at home there, I thought of the places as rooms, as extensions of the house itself. When he was in Greece I went off on my own. High up on the hill I had a secret hideout in an outcropping of rock. I kept my treasures in a small box, which I buried, dug up and reburied. My mother gave me a whistle to blow in case I needed help, but I always felt perfectly safe, as I never did in the city, even in the sanctity of Stuyvesant Town. In Kisco I felt part of the trees and bushes. It was as if I were inside a body, which was the earth itself, and my skin was no different from leaves. In the city, the earth was so well hidden under buildings and pavement it was easy to forget it was there at all. The few trees, the fenced areas of grass, were tamed specimens, deprived of soul.

After my grandfather defected to Athens, the house in Mt. Kisco became our weekend and summer home. It wasn't exactly a vacation spot. The neighbors lived there all year round and departed for the Cape or Maine as we took up residency in July. Our property taxes supported the extravagant Chappaqua school system, which I took advantage of only once, for a summer course in driver's ed with an instructor named Mr. Brightbill, who blew cigar smoke in our faces to get us used to driving under adverse conditions.

The Mt. Kisco house had been built for solidity, not casual living, a bourgeois fortress against the elements. The windows were all outfitted with aluminum venetian blinds like the bars on the Wards Island insane asylum. My mother kept them half lowered. The blinds across the big front picture window she kept all the way down, so people driving past couldn't see in. The house was set high enough above the road so even a Cyclops couldn't peer in, but my mother wasn't influenced by logic. In the dining room there was a back door with a small window also outfitted with a venetian blind. At every meal my father would yank it up, against my mother's protests. One lunchtime my father cried out, "I want my view." The view in question was a hillside covered with pachysandra, a rock stairway leading up to my grandfather's diminutive orchard. This time my father ripped the venetian blind right off its frame. The little window blinked like an eye that has had its blindfold torn off.

The next day a contractor turned up, and without much planning, the entire back wall was removed and replaced with sliding glass doors. It was the stylistic invasion of another decade, the early sixties imposing its taste on the spirit of the late forties.

It is not simply architecture that defines the difference in periods of style, but the way families relate to their outdoor space. When I was a little girl—the late forties and early fifties—everyone had screen porches or sunrooms. A filter was always between you and the outside air. In the later fifties and early sixties, everyone had a patio. They wanted to be outdoors now, close to the earth, preferably on flagstone or brick, or at least concrete. By the time I was a teenager the role of patios was being usurped by decks. Not content to adorn modern ranch houses they adhered themselves to any style of house they could. Across suburban New York conglomerations of redwood (later, green-tinged, pressure-treated wood) disfigured the backs and sides of Federal style homes, Capes, and Tudors. These great outdoor rooms were as underused as their predecessors.

We went to Mt. Kisco most weekends. We called the place— house and land—simply, Kisco. (The town was named for the

Algonquin Chief, Kisco, whose statue stood at a dangerous intersec-
tion.) In the summer we lived there full time and my father com-
muted to work in the city, mimicking the year-round life of his Mt.
Kisco neighbors. When my mother and I drove down to meet him at
the station at the end of the day he looked like those other commuter
fathers, the newspaper scrunched under his arm, though he never carried a briefcase, for what would a dentist put in one? One train ride
he complained to a seatmate, a year-round regular, that he felt like a
human yo-yo. The man was so taken by the phrase that it produced
an epiphany. He decided to give up the suburban life, with its hated
commute, and move back to the city.

In the front hall closet of our Stuyvesant Town apartment
resided the Himmelstein bag. This was a khaki-colored canvas duffel
bag, shaped like a baked potato, big enough so I could curl up inside
and zip it over my head. It had been World War II standard issue to
a friend of my parents, a doctor, whose name, Himmelstein, was imprinted on its side in imperfect black block letters. Dr. Himmelstein
died, not in The War, but still in his brilliant young manhood. I could
not conjure his face, but his bag was a regular part of my childhood,
and invoked him on every journey between Stuyvesant Town and the
country. All week long we put into the Himmelstein bag anything we
thought we might want to bring to Kisco. By Friday it was stuffed
with books and towels, sneakers and cereal boxes. When my father
went to get the car, my mother and I carried the bag in and out of the
elevator and outside the building, each taking one handle. When it
was heavy, we dragged it. My father slung it into the trunk of the car.
"What have you got in here, rocks?" he'd say.

At Kisco, the Himmelstein bag was unpacked and left in the
front hall closet. During the course of the weekend we filled it with
everything we wanted to bring back to Stuyvesant Town. This bag, a
survivor of The War, survived its new role for several decades: survived our yanking and dragging, survived the weather, survived my
humiliation. It looked like an article designed for camouflage, something left behind in a foxhole on a battlefield. It smelled like war. It

was not luggage, it was some enormous, ugly tumor we carried around with us. I would have liked matching leather luggage or copious wicker baskets. I would have liked to have made our exits and entrances in style.

But there was no style. If we looked, as my mother described us, like gypsies (though surely *their* bags would have been more colorful), she endured it. When we came back from Kisco we were usually additionally laden with sprays of fall leaves or cuttings of budding forsythia. My mother said she was always glad we didn't live in their old West Side apartment building where the doorman took a dim view of my parents' excursions to the country when they trailed through the lobby with muddy boots, foliage, fishing tackle, and, sometimes, dead fish. In Stuyvesant Town there was no scornful doorman in grey uniform with epaulets, there were only our neighbors, dressed in city attire, watching my mother and me dragging the Himmelstein bag up into the building and heaving it into the elevator.

Although my father never said so, we were in fact a family of human yo-yos, leading schizophrenic lives. There was always something incomplete, unfinished in the abode we had just left. We could not duplicate all our possessions, we had to divide or share. For the autobiography I wrote for a sixth-grade project, called *Town and Country Girl,* the cover picture was a self-portrait, split down the middle, blue jeans and braids on the side with trees, and the unmistakable brick rise of Stuyvesant Town in the background behind the half with pink dress and hairbows.

I wanted both; I could not imagine giving up either one. And yet there was a longing for a unified life, for a feeling that time wasn't always divided between here and there—for division of place makes division of time necessary, and brings a self-consciousness to it all. The clock is always hovering; time is always measured, not simply lived.

Mt. Kisco was upstream from Stuyvesant Town. We drove up the West Side Highway, against the current of the Hudson River, then up the Saw Mill River Parkway, against the current of that stream-sized river, its mills all erased or invisible. The Saw Mill River Parkway was indeed parklike, a pleasantly curving road that followed the river's meanders and was bordered with lawns and flowering trees. The speed limit was forty miles per hour. No one had seat belts. Weekends, many of the cars on the road had no destination at all. My father hated "Sunday drivers," and for the entire trip my mother focused on keeping him from honking, passing, and speeding.

At Kisco we were part of the natural order, witnesses to the vicissitudes of nature, as well as its victims. At Stuyvesant Town it was possible to go for days without going outside, to be as innocent of the weather or seasons as a person living in a space capsule. At Mt. Kisco the natural order created our schedules; we followed the necessities of seasons, the rhythms of day and night. In Stuyvesant Town time was an artificial ruler; our schedules kept their own pace, without a glimpse outside the window.

At Kisco we were the servants of nature's cycles: we raked leaves in the fall, shoveled snow in the winter, mowed the lawn in the summer. In Stuyvesant Town everything was done for us, we took no part in any seasonal maintenance. Battalions of men in brown uniforms made the leaves and the snow disappear, made the daffodils bloom and the lawns shimmer. All we had to take care of were our five small rooms: the cleaning, acquisition, and rearrangement of inanimate objects—which, strangely, was capable of occupying a life.

Our weekend retreats to Kisco were rarely relaxing. We had to Open the House, and then, when we left, Close the House. In addition to high-level cleaning (a mere grain of food left behind might result in colonies of ants) we had to fortify the house against possible break-ins. The house had been broken into several times, and each time it was the television set that was taken (the only thing of value). The good television set was raised by a system of pulleys (a creation of my father's) into the attic and in its place a decoy was substituted, an old set some Stuyvesant Town neighbor had discarded. One time the house had been broken into but nothing had been taken. It was only when the alarm clock went off at a predawn hour that my mother figured out some couple had been using the house as a romantic rendezvous.

We had seasonal rituals at Kisco. Cleaning gutters took up an entire weekend. Taking down storm windows took up another, as did putting them back up again. The house, left on its own all week, got into trouble in our absence, and our weekends were dedicated to setting things right. One week power had gone off and we arrived to find the refrigerator slimed over with black-green mold. One weekend we discovered mice had invaded the linen cabinet, where they had feasted on soap and nested in a box of sanitary napkins. We battled tent caterpillars one weekend, ants another weekend, and moles another. There were always trees to prune, underbrush to clear back, firewood to gather, gardens to weed, and if the outdoors relented for a week, we would plunge into sorting and cleaning projects in the garage, basement, or attic. Rarely did anything get thrown out.

Unlike Stuyvesant Town, where there were always lights outside at night, when night fell on Kisco it was darkness itself. I was aware of the habits of the moon, the vagaries of clouds. When the maple leaves were out, they muffled moon and stars; at night it was as if black blinds were drawn outside the windows. In my room, painted what was called "Corinne pink," my bed was under the window. In winter: cold air, fresh sheets (ironed smooth as paper at the Chinese laundry near Stuyvesant Town), a blanket that smelled always of moth balls. I listened to the house at night—branches against branches, branches scraping the roof edge—to the murmurs of the refrigerator, to the gurgles of water in the radiator. This warm water circulated around us like blood coursing through veins. The house was a living shell. Lying there in the silence of night, with the small noises of the house, I never thought about Stuyvesant Town at all, that other life. I had adjusted to the new time zone of Kisco, become my other self.

When we came back to Stuyvesant Town on Sunday there was always a letdown, a back-from-vacation feeling. The Himmelstein bag was filled with dirty laundry and my unfinished homework. Our apartment seemed shrunken, confining and ludicrously perched up in the air.

Gradually, though, the predictable ease of Stuyvesant Town asserted itself. There was limitless hot water in the bathtub. The toilet always flushed. There were no mice and no ants. Instead of the dirge of crickets or the rustling of leaves there were the sounds of our neighbors: pots clanking, bathtubs draining, doors closing, TVs murmuring, a couple quarreling, a mother nagging, a kid tap-dancing on a kitchen floor.

One Sunday when we returned to Stuyvesant Town from Kisco, my father, tired from a weekend of battling gypsy moths, embraced the livingroom wall and cried out "Ah! concrete and steel!" This became a standard litany upon our return to the apartment at the end of every weekend. Stuyvesant Town was that: All clean edges and straight lines. All lives tidy. Nature kept at bay.

*With my daughter on the monkey bars
in the "M" playground, 1993*

XXII

BRICKS

It was easy to think of Stuyvesant Town as a place where I happened to live, a temporary berth, but not a real home in the way that an actual house is. There was the basic difference between renting and owning—renting was like borrowing, owning (even if the true owner was the bank) was the real estate equivalent of immortality. And there was something fundamentally different between an apartment, a series of connected boxes high above the ground, and a house that was rooted in the earth. Stuyvesant Town was suited to transiency. Tenants left no permanent mark on the place. Once they moved on, their apartment was painted over in basic Stuyvesant Town beige and looked exactly as it did before they moved in; the plastic letters of their name in the hall directory didn't even leave a shadow behind.

Although for many residents Stuyvesant Town was just a place to live until they could afford to buy a home in Westchester or on the Island, many of the original tenants never moved. Some stayed because of financial considerations, others because they got used to the ways of Stuyvesant Town and found they had no desire to leave. There are mommies who sat on the benches forty years ago, watching their children in the playground, who sit on the same benches now and show each other pictures of their grandchildren. There are people who grew up in Stuyvesant Town who are now raising their own families there. It is possible that some of the children I grew up with in Stuyvesant Town will never live anywhere else. It is possible that Stuyvesant Town could grace an entire life.

When I left for college in the fall of 1964, I was setting my life on a path away from Stuyvesant Town, though I did not see it that way at the time. The assumption I started with—that I would end up back in New York, that I would be drawn back into Stuyvesant Town—waned over the years. I did come back to New York to go to graduate school, but Stuyvesant Town was a place I visited, a place to store the possessions of my past. I later lived in the Boston area, then the Pittsburgh area, then in Western Massachusetts, and with each move my habitat was progressively more rural, as if I were on a track that ran exactly counter to the course of urbanization. Perhaps it was Mt. Kisco that had irreversibly weakened Stuyvesant Town's hold on me, or at least given me enough of a taste of a different kind of life to facilitate conversion. As a girl I had pictured myself as straddling town and country; now I have stepped clearly over to one side. Even so, the word "home" invokes for me, still, the brick upon brick of Stuyvesant Town and our apartment "B," eleven stories high.

The kind of homes that I had believed were worthy of being written about, however, the kinds of homes that generated literary endeavors, were homesteads, farms, quaint villages or, if urban, neighborhoods that reveled in ethnic character. But a great many Americans don't have that heritage. We grew up in apartment buildings and housing projects, places that seem, at first glance, devoid of character.

I have left no trace of me behind at Stuyvesant Town, but Stuyvesant Town is still with me. Though it was homogeneous, symmetrical, and impersonal, it defined my childhood. It formed me, as it formed all of us who grew up there. A place like Stuyvesant Town, I've discovered, is a home, as much as any other.

Daffodils proliferate, all on their own. If you return to Stuyvesant Town in the springtime now after years away, you will be amazed how the sparse daffodils of your childhood have thrived and multiplied, great stretches of yellow, white, and gold drowning out the ivy. And the trees circling the Oval and stationed in front of your apartment have grown from saplings to presences as substantial as the buildings around them. Everything else from your childhood seems smaller now, diminished, but not these trees, not these flowers.

What else has changed in Stuyvesant Town? Most obviously, the habits of the residents, just as they have changed for the rest of the urban middle class. In the morning, men and women jog around the Oval before work. There is just a sprinkling of mommies sitting on the benches, most are off pursuing careers. Their preschool children are in day care or are watched over by nannies—some who take their places on the benches, next to the ranks of senior citizens. An annual flea market, where tenants can redistribute the detritus of their apartments (an activity formerly carried out discreetly through the local classifieds), is a popular event. The community seems more activist. Tenants organize not only for their rights, but to preserve the character of Stuyvesant Town as they see it. (Recently there was a tenants' rally against the installation of kiosks with vending machines.) One of the most notable changes in Stuyvesant Town is that it is now a racially integrated community. A lawsuit in the sixties, initiated by a committee of residents, forced the management to change its discriminatory policies. While the only black faces I saw regularly as a child were those of women employed to clean neighbors' apartments or look after their children, today Stuyvesant Town's residents more closely mirror the diversity of New York itself.

Stuyvesant Town does, though, still discriminate economically. There are minimum income level requirements for applicants. In 1999, for example, it was $51,000 gross annual income for a one-bedroom apartment in Stuyvesant Town (average rent: $1,150), $84,000 for one in Peter Cooper (average rent: $1,700). Prospective tenants are carefully screened. If homogeneity produces harmony, then Stuyvesant Town has achieved this by selecting tenants who can be expected to subscribe to the Stuyvesant Town mystique, though of course it can be argued only people who like Stuyvesant Town would choose to live there in the first place. And many do. Currently there is a two- to three-year estimated waiting time for one-bedroom apartments in Stuyvesant Town and so many applications on file for two-bedroom apartments that new ones are not even being accepted. Families living in two-bedroom Stuyvesant Town apartments can wait for years to move up to a coveted three-bedroom apartment, like mine.

Stuyvesant Town maintains its orderly character by assiduous maintenance, vigilant security, and rigorous tenant selection. The tenants are, on the whole, a law-abiding bunch, respectful of their neighbors, the grounds, and the buildings. There's no music blaring from the windows, garbage on the grass, or graffiti on the walls.

There are no statistics available to show the shifting demographics of the Stuyvesant Town population, but one observable difference between my time and the present is the aging of the residents. There weren't many older residents in Stuyvesant Town when I was a child—an occasional grandparent tucked in with the family, but rarely senior citizens living on their own.

Stuyvesant Town had been built for young families. It was a new town, and its first settlers were at the threshold of their own futures. A half-century later, their children grown and gone, many of the original settlers stayed on. While rents increased significantly each time an apartment turned over, rent stabilization laws ensured that the now-elderly Stuyvesant Town original residents could still afford their own apartments. It was not unusual for some to stay until they died.

I have heard Stuyvesant Town described as a "naturally occurring retirement community." It is certainly a haven now for the old. The recreation program caters to senior citizens now, not just children. A mild afternoon will bring out the most elderly residents—usually women—taking their cautious, babylike steps on the arm of a hired companion.

When I was growing up in Stuyvesant Town, we zipped around everywhere on bikes and roller skates. Today, in consideration of the numbers of senior citizens, bicycle riding and roller blading is prohibited. The blue metal Stuyvesant Town bicycle license plate is a relic of the past, and the one I've saved could probably fetch a tidy sum at the annual flea market.

The population of Stuyvesant Town has changed, but Stuyvesant Town itself has altered so little from the way I remembered it: new-style windows, the option of air- conditioners, new equipment in some of the playgrounds. My old playground seems at first untouched, but I discover one addition: thick rubber mats have been installed under the swings and under the monkey bars, where my childhood friends and I would climb, pretending we were in a castle or a spaceship or a tree.

The boxes, inexpertly taped, are stacked in the livingroom, awaiting the movers, the rugs are rolled and lassoed. The walls, stripped of their paintings, seem almost accusingly white. I look out the window across the Oval, pretend to myself that it is not the last time. The three spires of water in the fountain rise tall as the masts of a sailing ship. It is the first of May, and the trees all around the Oval are feathery with their pale, new-green leaves.

Before we leave Stuyvesant Town for good, though, there is something more I feel I have to do. I take my daughter downstairs with me to the "M" playground. We swing side by side, race each other down the "sliding ponds," and then head for the monkey bars. My daughter climbs on the structure alongside of me, and in an act of daring, I hang upside down from a cross bar where I dangled so many decades ago. I let go with my hands and grip with my knees. The metal is cold and slippery, familiar against my skin. I look at the upside down view of my old world, for a second, for a minute, for as long as I can brave it, and then I pull myself upright and catch my breath. I look at the apartment buildings around me once again.

In all these years, Stuyvesant Town itself seems not to have aged, except that the bricks seem to have softened. I don't know if this is actually possible. But it seems as if in a few decades the bricks have weathered so the edges are less sharp, and the shrill new-brick color has turned a softer red, the color of a red maple leaf just past its fall prime. Perhaps it's the contrast with the new buildings that have sprouted in Manhattan, taller, sharper-edged structures of steel and glass. Or perhaps it is just a trick of light.

My father, age 70

Epilogue

During the time I was working on this book, my father was diagnosed with cancer. He died a few months later. I had dedicated the book to him and had hoped he would live to see it in its finished form. He had read the first manuscript version, making small corrections and laughing—to my great relief—at anecdotes about our past life together in Stuyvesant Town.

I have chosen not to rewrite the parts that deal with my father most recently, but to leave him, as he had been when I wrote this memoir, alive, in the present tense.

Corinne Demas is the author of two collections of short stories, *What We Save For Last* and *Daffodils or the Death of Love,* a novel, *The Same River Twice,* and numerous books for children, including *Matthew's Meadow* and *If Ever I Return Again.* Her publications before 2000 are under the name Corinne Demas Bliss. A graduate of Tufts University, she has a Ph.D. in English and Comparative Literature from Columbia University. She is a Professor of English at Mt. Holyoke College and a fiction editor of *The Massachusetts Review.* For more information about the author and *Eleven Stories High: Growing Up in Stuyvesant Town, 1948–1968,* visit her web site, www.corinnedemas.com.

DATE DUE

HIGHSMITH #45230

Printed
in USA